A HISTORY OF BLACK CONGREGATIONAL CHRISTIAN CHURCHES OF THE SOUTH

A History of Black Congregational Christian Churches of the South

by
J. Taylor Stanley

Limited Edition
Published by United Church Press
for the American Missionary Association

United Church Press, 287 Park Avenue South, New York, New York 10010

To
my wife, Kathryn, who was the "Gypsy" of my wanderings
and who shared my total commitment to Christ and my years
of ministry to the Convention of the South,
and to
the ministers, women, men, and young people across the South,
whose constant friendship, loyalty, devotion, and service
to the Black Congregational Christian Churches renewed
my own
faith and gave me an experience in churchmanship that was
"a thing of beauty and a joy forever"

Contents

Foreword

The Black church within the United Church of Christ is a mirror reflecting all the ways in which the UCC and its predecessor bodies responded to the varied changes of the larger society. The classical American Dilemma, from the very beginning of the nation, at Jamestown and Plymouth, has been the anguished adoption of the Christian conscience to pervasive racism. The history of the Black church within the United Church of Christ is the story of that dilemma.

How fortunate we are that J. Taylor Stanley has taken the time to record this fascinating chronicle. He is probably the only one who could have done it for our time. He is providentially equipped with both the experience and the irenic spirit to write the record. His experience spans the Congregational-Christian merger, the transition of Black church work from the time of the American Missionary Association to a more regularized church extension program within the consolidated home mission agency, and the formation of the United Church of Christ. These three periods form the facets of this UCC mirror of the American Dilemma.

Dr. Stanley had his spiritual and intellectual origins with the American Missionary Association. He embodies the social and spiritual ideals of that great institution. He also embodies some of its dilemmas. Dr. Stanley was a product of an AMA school, where the dominant influence was New England Congregationalism. This whole movement was a "missionary movement" to bring spiritual and intellectual enlightenment to the benighted. In retrospect, this movement can easily be caricatured, and often has been, as a well-meaning attempt of middle-class New Englanders to teach primitive Black folk how to "act white." But the presence of a J. Taylor Stanley in our midst exposes that caricature as a shallow misunderstanding of the AMA era. The AMA responded to the desperate need of the postemancipation period with a demonstration of the equality of Black people. It chose to demonstrate that Black people were fully capable of participating in the highest and best forms of education society had to offer. Unfortunately, this education had inextricable social class overtones, but there were the J. Taylor Stanleys who could and did translate from one culture to another, thereby making possible the demonstration of equality and preserving the respect for Black culture at the same time.

The merger of the Congregationalists and the Christians brought the AMA Blacks into contact with the uneducated, primitive Black Christians of a different social class. This merger challenged all the skills Dr. Stanley had in order to bring some kind of unity and common identity to the Black Congregational Christians. Even though that merger idea originated a long distance outside the Black church community, in retrospect, it had many constructive results, which Dr. Stanley's history describes.

Dr. Stanley's leadership of the Convention of the South (as the Black Congregational Christians were called) was a remarkable achievement under tremendous obstacles of geography and class distinctions. He, almost alone, shaped a new identity for these churchpeople and made Black Congregational Christians a respected part of the Congregational Christian Churches.

Then came the next merger; again an idea originated at considerable distance from the Convention of the South. Since there were no Black Evangelical and Reformed churches to merge into the Convention of the South, it was decided the time had come to dissolve the convention and integrate the churches into various conferences. Thus, the Convention of the South was divided among the Southern, Central Atlantic, Southeast, Indiana-Kentucky, Missouri, and South Central conferences. Again, the United Church of Christ illustrated the painful American Dilemma. Just as the Black churches were beginning to develop a sense of identity they were fragmented and distributed among UCC structures. It was predictable that some new organizational entity representing Black churches would come into being in the United Church of Christ.

Dr. Stanley has illuminated for all of us this continuing story of a church within a church. In his account he has described all the anguish and pain as well as the moments of triumph and glory that make up the human fabric of the many strands that form the United Church of Christ. Through his book the entire fellowship may be able to understand a little more clearly the meaning of pluralism.

Wesley A. Hotchkiss

Acknowledgments

The people who have given me assistance and encouragement in writing this history of Black Congregational Christian churches in the South are too numerous to name. I am appreciative of the many letters, historical sketches of churches, occasional scraps of old church records and special church programs, and a few good pictures. I also had many informative conversations with individuals. I am especially grateful to a few persons, however, who deserve special mention: Oma W. Johnson, Dr. Durwood T. Stokes, and the librarian at Elon College, for access to the Church History Room and for considerable assistance in locating the very illusive materials concerning Afro-Christian churches; the librarian and her assistants at Talladega College, who made my days among the archives of the library very fruitful ones, to the extent that there I had my first real insight into the beginnings of Congregationalism among Black people in the South; Dr. Clifton H. Johnson, director of the Amistad Research Center at Dillard University, and the lovely young women who work at the center for a wonderful guided week of exploration through minutes, reports, and files of the American Missionary Association, from the origin of the association to the mid-twentieth century, and for their painstaking copying of hundreds of pages selected from these files; Dr. Wesley A. Hotchkiss, the Rev. Edwin M. Alcorn, Dr. Percel O. Alston, and Dr. James H. Lightbourne Jr. for their encouragement and prodding and for their generous financial assistance. Special mention should be made of the Rev. Junious O. Lee, Suffolk, Virginia; the Rev. John P. Mangrum, Franklinton, North Carolina; the Rev. Claude C. Simmons, New Bern, North Carolina; Dr. Homer C. McEwen, Atlanta, Georgia; and the Rev. John T. Enwright, Charleston, South Carolina; also Seth T. Shaw, Kenly, North Carolina; Dr. Howard M. Jason, Savannah, Georgia; Robert C. Johnson, Birmingham, Alabama; Elgin Hychew, Houston, Texas; Enlar Brown, Newport News, Virginia; Hortense Boone, Holland, Virginia; Vina W. Webb, Sedalia, North Carolina; Siddie C. Greene, Merritt, North Carolina;

Charlotte Greene, Raleigh, North Carolina; Eliza Durham, Manson, North Carolina; Merlissie Ross Middleton, Atlanta, Georgia; Selica Jones, Anniston, Alabama; Mildred W. Newton; Daisy Young and Lillian Dunn, New Orleans. All these, and many others in lesser degree, have shared with me old conference minutes, news clippings, letters, pictures, special church programs, and delightful conversations about their churches, their ministers, and their own experiences in the work of the church. To all these people I am deeply grateful. Also, I owe special thanks to Mr. and Mrs. Robert N. Perry, New Orleans, Louisiana, and to Mr. and Mrs. Rufus Greene, Merritt, North Carolina, for extended days of hospitality in their homes and for transportation and guidance to points of interest in their areas. All together, concerned friends of our Black churches of the South helped to make it possible for me to piece together the information contained in this book. My daughters, Bettye and Joye, have merited special praise and thanks for the patience with which they have gone through the rough manuscript I had produced and have transformed it into presentable copy.

Further, it will be noted that there are no footnotes or list of references in this book, except as indicated in the text. Such footnotes and catalog of references would be next to impossible to include. I have limited correspondence and reports from the files of Dr. Alfred Lawless; considerably more from the files of the Rev. Henry S. Barnwell; and, of course, a mass of such materials from my own files. In addition, there are many minutes of meetings of association, conferences, women's conventions, Sunday school conventions of the Convention of the South, as well as minutes and reports of the Convention of the South itself; many church programs, news clippings, and notes on conversations that I have engaged in across the field. In due time I hope to offer all this accumulation of materials to the Church History Room in the library of Elon College, the archives of the library of Talladega College, or to the Amistad Research Center at Dillard University.

Beyond this I have found the following books and reports to be very helpful resource material: *A Crusade of Brotherhood: A History of the American Missionary Association* by Augustus F.

Beard; *A History of the Christian Denomination in America* by Milo T. Morrill; *New Day Ascending* by Fred L. Brownlee; *American Missionary, The Christian Annual,* the *Annual Reports of the American Missionary Association,* year books of the Congregational Churches, the Congregational Christian Churches, and the United Church of Christ.

J.T.S.

About the Author

J. Taylor Stanley has had a long and interesting career as a minister of the Congregational Christian churches of the South. After graduation from the School of Religion at Howard University, Washington, D.C., he moved to his first pastorate, the Howard Church, of Nashville, Tennessee. While in Nashville he married the former Kathryn M. Turrentine, who came from a Congregational family of long history and who had served as the first Black church extension worker in the South. They are the parents of five children: Joseph Jr. (deceased), Thomas W., Joye, Bettye, and A. Knighton.

From Nashville the Stanleys moved to North Carolina to serve Gregory Church in Wilmington. After two and a half years in Wilmington the family moved to the farming community of Dudley, North Carolina, to the First Congregational Church. The family grew from two in Nashville to four in Wilmington to seven in Dudley and shared fully in the community life of Dudley and the surrounding areas.

Many feel that Dudley was Dr. Stanley's most successful and enjoyable pastorate. During the Depression years he built a beautiful church edifice, which became the nerve center of the community and around which everything else revolved. This work became well known and attracted visitors from neighboring localities and from the regional and national offices of the Congregational Christian denomination. While still in Dudley, Dr. Stanley was urged to teach in the ministers' institute at Franklinton Center, in North Carolina. Later, he was asked to become the director of rural church work in North Carolina and in Virginia, and while serving in this capacity he had an opportunity to work with the former Christian churches of these two states, which had merged with the former Congregational churches. In the process Dr. Stanley established rapport with the Black Christians in their Sunday school conventions, conferences, and retreats and in the local churches. This made him a natural for working with them as their superintendent. He developed a sensitivity for them, their programs, and their needs that he could articulate to the former Congregational churches, whose background he already knew.

As testimony to his successful pastorate at Dudley, his effective ministry with the town and country churches of North Carolina and of Virginia, his deep understanding of all facets of church life, his commitment and ability to relate to people, Dr. Stanley was elected to the superintendency of the Black Congregational Christian churches of the South. He served exceptionally well in this position until his retirement.

Since his retirement he has served with distinction as interim director of Dorchester Center, McIntosh, Georgia and of Franklinton Center, Bricks, North Carolina; and as interim pastor and builder of the Congregational United Church of Christ, High Point, North Carolina.

Merlissie Ross Middleton

Chapter 1

Introduction

The history of the Black Congregational Christian churches in the South covers a short span of 110 years, from 1865 to 1975. During this period these churches, springing from two separate sources in parallel streams, have had their romantic beginnings, their golden years of achievement and expansion, and their heartbreaking years of decline brought on by wars, migrations, the Depression, and changing patterns in southern social, economic, cultural, and religious structures.

I have lived through more than three fourths of these 110 years. For over sixty-five years, through schools, colleges, seminary, and churches as student, pastor, and superintendent of Negro Congregational Christian churches in the South, I have been intimately related to Congregationalism and to Congregational Christian churches since the merger in 1931. Because I have known personally many prominent Black leaders of both traditions and have visited most of the churches under consideration, much of this story may be considered an eyewitness account of my own experiences and services among these leaders and churches.

My involvement with the work of the denomination began in the fall of 1907, when, at nine years of age, I became the youngest boarding student at Lincoln Normal School, in Marion, Alabama. Also, I was probably the most "country," the most homesick, and, at times, the most hungry of the students. This was a whole new experience for me: to be warmed by a heater fired with something other than wood; to use toilet facilities (although still out of doors); to sit at a school desk (mine was third-grade size!); to be associated with and taught by white persons, to be respected by them and, when I was the most homesick, to be lifted to their laps and given reassurance of tenderness and love and of belonging. It was at this time that I attended a Congregational Sunday school and church service for the first time. My Sunday school teacher was also one of my teachers at Lincoln

Normal School. The church service was orderly; the sermon was quiet and informative. Offerings were received by passing plates, and no appeal was made for second-round giving "to make out $5.00 even," or six if we exceeded five. The Rev. Thomas L. Routt was pastor of the church and chaplain in charge of the morning chapel services held at the school each day. Many, many years later it was my privilege to return to the chapel of Lincoln Normal School and to give the eulogy in the funeral services for the Reverend Routt; and still later, to go to Lexington, Kentucky for the funeral services of his widow.

After leaving Lincoln Normal School I had smatterings of training at Bibb County Training School, Centreville, Alabama, from which I graduated in the class of 1918; at Talladega College, Talladega, Alabama; at Howard University and at the School of Religion of Howard University, Washington, D.C., from which I graduated in the class of 1925; and at Fisk University, Nashville, Tennessee. All these institutions, except Bibb County Training School, were founded by and supported wholly or in part by the American Missionary Association.

After graduation from seminary I was ordained to the Christian ministry on July 9, 1925, in Lincoln Memorial Congregational Church, Washington, D.C. and was called to my first pastorate the same month. I served three churches as pastor before becoming associate superintendent in charge of Negro church work in the southeastern district of Congregational Christian churches and later, superintendent of the Convention of the South.

My Three Pastorates

Howard Congregational Church, Nashville, Tennessee, 1925–29. This church was named for Maj. Gen. O.O. Howard. The property was owned by the American Missionary Association. Originally, the church building, an impressive bit of Gothic architecture, served as the Fisk University Chapel and had towered majestically over the army barracks that domiciled Fisk University in its initial years. The church was still referred to as the Howard Chapel.

Gregory Congregational Church, Wilmington, North Carolina, 1929–31. My wife and I arrived in Wilmington in April 1929. There were four buildings: the parsonage, which was rented out in exchange for janitorial services; and the three Gregory Institute buildings—the church, the teachers' home, and the rambling two-story frame schoolhouse. The church had been struck by lightning, brickbats, and broken glass, and other debris covered the sidewalk and littered the yard; windows were boarded up, and exposed framework provided an inviting roosting place for pigeons. We were housed in the old teachers' home, then known as the Gregory Community Center. The first week we were there the chief of the Wilmington Fire Department informed us that the building was condemned, but upon urgent appeal he granted us thirty days to either put the building in acceptable condition or move out. The first weeks at Gregory were spent with carpenters, painters, and other workers as they rebuilt porches and steps, reglazed the equivalent of nineteen large windows, painted new and old outside woodwork, and replaced or restored gas, electric, and plumbing lines and fixtures. As a result of this renovation, we did not have to move. My very pregnant wife managed to live through this ordeal, and our first child was born in the center ten weeks after our arrival in Wilmington.

The old schoolhouse was condemned at the close of the school year and was never used again. Much of the rest of my two and a half years at Wilmington was taken up with rebuilding the church steeple and the front end of the church, placing new windows in the church, repairing and refinishing the interior of the community center, and getting the old schoolhouse removed from the premises. At the same time, we were working toward having well-rounded religious and recreational programs for the church and the community.

First Congregational Christian Church, Dudley, North Carolina, 1931–42. The Stanley family moved from Wilmington to Dudley on October 1, 1931. Our first residence was a white-owned tenant house that had served as a storage place for potatoes. A few potatoes and most of the smell of rotting potatoes remained in the house. We soon moved into a slightly better house, which was owned by a member of the church. We lived there until

3

construction on our own house was far enough along for us to move in.

Dudley, a farm community, was deep in the throes of the Great Depression. The church site consisted of eleven acres of land that belonged to the American Missionary Association. The cemetery and the second two-room school-church building erected here by the AMA occupied a portion of this site. The rest was woodland. The call to Dudley was accepted on condition that full-time pastoral service would be provided, and that the church would be moved into the center of the community that it served. Within ninety days we had found and purchased a two-acre corner lot located at the crossroads near the heart of the village. Church and pastor each bought one half of this site.

The old church building was well built and well preserved. Its main timbers were mortised and tied together with one-inch wooden pins. The seats were made on the lot and had collapsible desk-backs, which served the school on weekdays but which allowed freedom for standing at worship services and special meetings. (Some of these seats are preserved in the new church.) The people of Dudley were depressed and poor, but they were ready and eager to follow leadership, to make sacrifices, and to participate in the building of a new church and in the development of a unique rural church program. The first step was to take down the old building and to move salvageable material to the new site. The new church was built almost entirely by local effort and local finance. (A grant of $500 was the extent of financial aid received from the denomination.) At least 95 percent of labor required was contributed freely by bricklayers, carpenters, plasterers, and other workers in the community; the church was debt-free when completed. A fenced playground offered a tennis court and a variety of recreational equipment. Through the generosity of northern friends, the library was furnished with hundreds of books. The work being done at Dudley attracted the attention of many denominational workers, as well as a number of friends from surrounding towns and communities. Also, the uniqueness of our efforts as a rural parish was a training ground and a stepping-stone for future duties.

While still pastor at Dudley I accepted the part-time position of director of rural church work in North Carolina and in Virginia, and for four years I served the town and country churches of these two states, attending all conference, association, and convention meetings and working, usually as an instructor, in summer conferences, youth camps, ministers' institutes, and a variety of retreats and workshops whenever and wherever they were held. During this period I visited nearly every rural church in the area and became acquainted with the ministers and lay leaders of these churches. There was no salary connected with the position and the $40 per month that was allowed for expenses was more than used up by travel. However, this work with rural churches was a rewarding and wonderful experience, which more than any other one thing prepared me for my later work as superintendent of the Convention of the South. Three fourths of all the Negro churches in the South and about the same percentage of membership were in small towns and in rural communities; 80 percent of these Black churches were in North Carolina and in Virginia. Getting to know these churches and learning to work with their pastors, lay leaders, and young people afforded invaluable background training for me.

On Sunday afternoon, March 1, 1942, Superintendent Henry S. Barnwell died of a heart attack. The preceding Thursday and Friday we were in meeting together in Winston-Salem, North Carolina, where the demands of leadership required much of his wisdom and ingenious directives as well as his physical strength. Saturday he drove through Greensboro, Burlington, and Mebane, to Strieby, North Carolina, calling on friends along the way. He arrived at the St. Luke Church, Goldston, North Carolina, in time for Sunday school and the morning worship service, at which he delivered the sermon. He spent the afternoon visiting friends and churches in the Sanford vicinity and was scheduled to return to the St. Luke Church for the evening service. He did not arrive; he died on the road. His plan was to visit with me in Dudley on Monday, March 2, to complete details of our trip together to a special denominational meeting in Philadelphia. His dream of uniting all Black Congregational Christian churches of the South into a strong conference remained unfulfilled. He had given his life to his work beyond his physical endurance. He had labored untiringly and zealously at a thankless, frustrating, impossible job during the most crucial years perhaps for the Negro churches in the South.

This was the impossible job I was persuaded to take by a committee of nine, consisting of three Negro Congregationalists —the Rev. William J. Faulkner, the Rev. Norman A. Holmes, and the Rev. Henry Curtis McDowell; three Afro-Christians— the Rev. Joseph D. Farrar, the Rev. F.A. Hargett, and the Rev. Charles A. Harris; the Rev. William T. Scott, superintendent of the Southeast District; the Rev. Ernest M. Haliday and the Rev. Thomas A. Tripp, of the Extension Division of the Board of Home Missions. During the meeting of the General Council of Congregational Christian Churches, in Durham, New Hampshire, the committee to elect a successor to superintendent Barnwell, after several sessions, had eliminated other nominations and applications and had settled upon me as their selection for the post.

Two hundred thirty-five churches were listed in my new parish. One hundred sixty-seven of these churches were concentrated in North Carolina and in Virginia. The remaining sixty-eight churches were scattered over ten other southern states and included a migratory spillover of five churches in New Jersey and in New York. One hundred twenty-nine churches in the district were of Afro-Christian background; 106 were Congregational.* This unwieldy parish extended from Yorktown, Virginia to Corpus Christi, Texas, from Charleston, South Carolina to Oklahoma City, Oklahoma, from Louisville, Kentucky to Beachton, Georgia, and provided happy "hunting ground" in New Jersey and in New York.

At the beginning of my ministry as superintendent there were thirteen conferences or associations, and each had separate women's conventions or departments and Sunday school conventions or youth departments. Several associations had at least three separate annual meetings; a few had midyear sessions. Each annual session held forth from three to five days. There

* All figures from 1942 *Year Book,* Congregational Christian Churches.

were twenty-five to thirty of these annual meetings, and the superintendent was expected (if not required) to put in an appearance and to deliver an address at each one. In addition, there were five conference centers, with a youth conference or camp at each center each summer, and annual institutes for ministers, church school workers, women, and men at those centers that had housing and heating facilities. The superintendent shared in the planning of programs, the selection of staff personnel, and usually served as director and business administrator of all church-related activities at these centers. Add to this the normal duties and responsibilities of a conference superintendent and you have all the makings of an overwhelming assignment.

This was worsened by the changing attitudes of the Church Extension Division of the Board of Home Missions regarding the number of staff persons a conference superintendent needed. Mr. Barnwell had a full-time office secretary, a director of Christian education, two assistant directors of Christian education, and a part-time director of rural church work in North Carolina and in Virginia. Within a year after I assumed the position my staff was reduced to a combination office secretary-director of religious education. The budget was cut and rigidly controlled. Our two salaries were set at $2,750 and $1,200 per year. All other expenses were limited and were exceeded at our own risk. How we had to skimp! We welcomed good or bad free entertainment in homes, gifts of food supplies, and sometimes cash gifts, which we were not allowed to accept.

This was the job that I accepted and at which I worked for twenty-three years. During those years I visited nearly every one of the 235 churches, even the inactive ones. I have personally known almost all the pastors and their spouses, especially those who came into the ministry of our church because of my persuasion and choosing. I have shared their hardships and griefs, their joys and successes, both of ministers and of churches. I have preached at least once practically every Sunday of these twenty-three years and often on weekdays and special occasions. I have lived and identified with these ministers and churches throughout these years.

Out of this background, rich in personal experiences, a dramatic history unfolds. To a large extent it is an eyewitness account, for I have played a significant role in the drama. For this I make no apology.

Also, I make no claim to glowing achievement; no miracles were performed. Many problems remained unsolved. Many hopes remained unfulfilled. Although it was slow, there was measurable and gratifying progress made in the quantity and quality of dedicated ministerial and lay leadership, in the growth of church and church school enrollment, in improved church buildings and facilities, in financial support, and especially, in an improved attitude toward the office of superintendent and improved relationships between different economic, cultural, and religious backgrounds in the Black churches of the South.

The account that follows is the story of Black Congregational Christians being discovered and called out by white Congregationalists and white Christians and of Blacks discovering themselves and their need for Christ, for spiritual enlightenment, and for the dynamics of their involvement in the life and work of the church. This new awakening helped to make possible the organization of all Black Congregational Christian churches in the South into the Convention of the South.

Chapter 2

Beginnings of Congregationalism
Among Southern Blacks

No history of Negro Congregational churches in the South can be written without bold reference to the work of the American Missionary Association with Negroes before, during, and after the Civil War.

Early in 1846 a call for a convention was sent out to "Friends of Bible Missions." The convention was held in Albany, New York in September. The call stated that "the time has come when those who would sustain missions for the propagation of a pure and free Christianity should institute arrangements for gathering and sustaining churches in heathen lands, from which the sins of caste, polygamy, slave-holding and the like shall be excluded." After two days of open discussion the American Missionary Association was formed. First officers elected included the Honorable William Jackson, of Massachusetts, president; the Rev. George Whipple, of Ohio, corresponding secretary; and Lewis Tappan, of New York, treasurer. The association was incorporated in the State of New York on January 30, 1849. The original constitution of the American Missionary Association indicated the firmness of its intent and the nature of its mission:

Article I.   This Society shall be called "THE AMERICAN MISSIONARY ASSOCIATION."

Article II.   The object of this Society shall be to send the Gospel to those portions of our own and other countries which are destitute of it, or which present open and urgent fields of effort.

Article III. Any person of evangelical sentiments, who professes faith in the Lord Jesus Christ, who is not a slave-holder, or in the practice of other immoralities, and who contributes to the funds, may become a member of the Society; and by payment of thirty dollars, a life member; provided, that children and others who have not professed their faith, may become life members without the privilege of voting.

Article IV. This Society shall meet annually in the month of September, October or November, for the election of officers and the transaction of other business at such time and place as shall be designated by the Executive Committee.

Article V. The Annual meeting shall be constituted of the officers and members of the Society at the time of such meeting, and of delegates from churches, local missionary societies, and other cooperating bodies—each body being entitled to one representative.

Article VI. The officers of the Society shall be a President, Vice-Presidents, a Recording Secretary, Corresponding Secretaries, Treasurer, two Auditors, and an Executive Committee of not less than 12, of which the Corresponding Secretaries and Treasurer shall be ex-officio members.

Article VII. To the Executive Committee shall belong the collecting and disbursing of funds; the appointing, counseling, sustaining, and dismissing (for just and sufficient reasons) missionaries and agents; the selecting of missionary fields; and, in general, the transaction of all such business as usually appertains to the executive committee of missionary or other benevolent societies; the Committee to exercise no ecclesiastical jurisdiction over the missionaries; and its doings to be subject always to the revision of the annual meeting, which shall, by a reference mutually chosen, always entertain the complaints of any aggrieved agent or missionary;

and the decision of such reference shall be final.

The Executive Committee shall have authority to fill all vacancies occurring among the officers between the regular annual meetings; to apply, if they see fit, to any State Legislature for acts of incorporation where any is given, of all officers, agents, missionaries, or others in the employment of the Society; to make provision, if any, for disabled missionaries, and for the widows and children of such as are deceased; and to call in all parts of the country, at their discretion, special and general conventions of the friends of missions, with a view to the diffusion of the missionary spirit, and the general and vigorous support of the Missionary work.

Five members of the Committee shall constitute a quorum for transacting business.

Article VIII. This Society, in collecting funds, in appointing officers, agents and missionaries, and in selecting fields of labor, and conducting the missionary work, will endeavor particularly to discountenance slavery, by refusing to receive the known fruits of unrequited labor, or welcome to its employment those who hold their fellow-beings as slaves.

Article IX. Missionary bodies, churches, or individuals agreeing to the principles of this Society, and wishing to appoint and sustain missionaries of their own, shall be entitled to do so through the agency of the Executive Committee, on terms mutually agreed upon.

Article X. No amendment shall be made in this Constitution without the concurrence of two thirds of the members present at a regular annual meeting; nor unless the proposed amendment has been presented to a previous meeting, or to the Executive Committee in session to be published by them (as it shall be their duty to do, if so submitted), in the regular official notification of the meeting.

This constitution is presented in its entirety, as it was published in the early issues of the *American Missionary,* the monthly journal of the American Missionary Association. It leaves no doubt as to the opposition of the association to human slavery and as to its commitment to its mission to carry Christian enlightenment to the oppressed and the disadvantaged of all races. At its fourth annual meeting, in 1850, the association passed this resolution:

Resolved, that we believe the Christianity of the nation is about to be tested, in view of the late act of Congress for the recovery of fugitive slaves, which appears equally at variance with the principles of the Association, the Constitution of the country, and the law of God, and that as Christians we do solemnly covenant with each other and our colored brethren that we cannot obey it, nor any law that contravenes the higher law of our Maker, whatever persecution or penalty we may be called to suffer.

Perhaps the greatest issue that confronted the United States from its beginning was the question of slavery. It became a real issue in the Constitutional Convention of 1787, and it became a problem of conscience for many, even some of the South's representatives, who had worked from May to September to help hammer out the Constitution of the United States. (The South demanded that slaves, although not citizens, should be counted in the population of the slave states.) Thomas Jefferson, the most outspoken of the antislavery slaveholders, in discussing slavery, said, "I tremble for my country when I reflect that God is Just." In 1784, in his *Notes on the State of Virginia,* Jefferson recommended "that the slaves be purchased by the Government and sent to form a colony in the West Indies." Although he failed in his attempt to persuade Congress to exclude slavery from all territory west of the Alleghenies, under the Ordinance of 1787, slavery was prohibited from the Northwest Territory. John Randolph stated "that all other misfortunes of [his] life were small compared with being born a master of slaves." In his will Randolph liberated all his slaves. In a letter to his secretary, Tobias Lear, George Washington wrote that he was anxious to "dispose of a certain kind of property as soon as possible." The property referred to was Negro slaves. In 1817 a colonization society was founded and received strong southern support.. Its purpose was to establish the free Negroes of the nation as a colony in Liberia, on the west coast of Africa. Antislavery societies existed in such slaveholding states as Delaware, Virginia, North Carolina, Kentucky, and Tennessee before any such societies were formed in New England. By 1826 there were 144 antislavery societies, 106 of which were in the South. Ten years later there was no such society in the South.

During this decade slavery became the hottest and most divisive issue in the nation, between North and South. The battle lines were drawn; the seeds for civil war were sown, although twenty-five years would lapse before the harvest. The issues were apparent everywhere—in politics, in churches, in homes and society, and in agriculture, industry, and commerce. Slavery was unprofitable to the North; it was considered essential to the cotton economy of the South. The Missouri Compromise and other compromises affecting slavery, before and after, generated long and heated arguments in both houses of Congress. Laws were flaunted, and slaves were moved into the Southwest and across the Ohio River into southern Illinois and Indiana. At the same time, underground railroads, abolitionist organizations, and many sympathetic individuals helped fugitive slaves and "free" Negroes to escape into Canada or to establish residence beyond the reach of their masters.

Although most Congregationalists were strongly united in their opposition to slavery during the first half of the nineteenth century, some were divided on the issue; the majority were antislavery rather than abolitionists. They were at the forefront with others who denounced slavery and helped tremendously in bringing about its overthrow. There are names that stand out.

In January 1831 William Lloyd Garrison published the first issue of *The Liberator,* in which he began his attack on Negro slavery, an attack that continued relentlessly until the close of the Civil War. In 1845 Joseph W. Thompson moved from Chapel

Street Church, New Haven, Connecticut, to become pastor of Broadway Tabernacle in New York City. Richard S. Storrs was called to the pastorate of the Church of the Pilgrims in Brooklyn, New York in 1846. A new Congregational enterprise, which became the Plymouth Church in Brooklyn, called Henry Ward Beecher to be its first pastor. Not only were these men great contemporary pastors and preachers in the largest urban community in the country, but they were also quite dedicated and vocal in their fight against slavery.

Leonard Bacon, in 1846, published a book titled *Slavery Discussed.* The book had wide circulation, and in later years Abraham Lincoln referred to it as the source of his clear convictions concerning slavery—convictions that prompted him to issue the Emancipation Proclamation on January 1, 1863. In 1851 *Uncle Tom's Cabin,* written by Harriet Beecher Stowe, was serialized in a Washington journal, *The National Era.* The story stirred the hearts of many people, from Maine to California, and made the execution of the new Fugitive Slave Law impossible. It did more than any other one thing to break down all barriers to the emancipation of the slaves.

Speaking of her father, Lyman Beecher, Harriet Beecher Stowe once said she could never forget the effect his preaching and daily prayers had upon her life—"prayers offered with strong, crying tears, which indelibly impressed my heart and made me what I am from my very soul, the enemy of slavery. Every brother I have has been in his own sphere a leading antislavery man."

Lewis and Arthur Tappan and Joshua Leavitt were among those who organized the American Antislavery Society in 1833. Nearly all its charter members were also enrolled in churches and included Congregationalists, Presbyterians, Quakers, Unitarians, and members of other denominations. Arthur Tappan was elected president of the society. By 1837 this society was comprised of twelve hundred auxiliary societies and a membership of about 125,000. At the seventh annual meeting of the society, in 1840, the body divided, as expected, and a new national body, the American and Foreign Antislavery Society, was formed. Arthur Tappan was also chosen to head this organization.

The Tappan brothers played a significant part in establishing and supporting the American Missionary Association. The task of the AMA was clear-cut; the time was never more ripe for the work the association had set its mind to do—to carry the spirit of the gospel of Jesus Christ, education, and physical relief to the underprivileged and the exploited, to those who were denied the rights of human freedom and human dignity. Much of the activity centered along the boundaries between North and South. To the north, routes of escape for runaway slaves developed, and sympathetic ministers, churches, and others provided food, shelter, and transportation to free states in the North and the West and into Canada. Thousands of slaves got away through these underground railroads. Some Negroes bought their freedom and, occasionally, the freedom of their parents or children or companions. Sometimes compassionate masters freed their slaves. Although most of these freedmen remained in the South, there were many who went north. It is estimated that by 1860 there were nearly 500,000 free Negroes in America, over half of them in slave-owning states. Even Mississippi recorded close to one thousand free Negroes.

In its early years the American Missionary Association extended its work to foreign fields—Africa, the West Indies, Siam, and among the Copts in Egypt and the refugees from slavery in Canada. Within twenty-five years almost all foreign missions had been discontinued or had been turned over to the American Board of Commissioners for Foreign Missions. (The African missions of the AMA went to the United Brethren and met until 1882.)

There was a crying need for home missions. The question of slavery had thrust the country into crisis and had created a divisiveness between North and South that has not yet been healed. Also, it provided the American Missionary Association with its greatest opportunity for service on home fields. This service was rendered during the most trying times and under the most difficult circumstances. The association established missions in Ohio, Michigan, Indiana, Illinois, Wisconsin, and as far west as Minnesota and Iowa. A special purpose of these missions was to promote sentiment against slavery and the sin of caste. Southern missions of the association had the distinction of being the first to organize churches and schools on a strictly antislavery basis.

A good example of the unswerving Christian commitment of the missionaries is found in the action of the Rev. John G. Fee, of Kentucky. Fee, the son of a slaveholder, was disinherited by his father because of his convictions regarding slavery. After completing his theological studies in Cincinnati, he spent several years with the American Home Missionary Society but withdrew from the AHMA because of its refusal to disfellowship slaveholders from its churches. He then applied to the American Missionary Association and was commissioned on October 10, 1848. He returned to Kentucky and for several years continued to preach and to organize antislavery churches. The following statements from letters written to the American Missionary Association during these years witness to his enthusiasm and zeal:

[1849] Our congregations are regularly increasing in size and interest. The general impression through the community now is that an antislavery church can exist and prosper in a slave state.

[1854] A whole gospel can be preached in the South, and churches having no fellowship with slavery are organized and have fair prospects of success.

[1859] We need a college here which shall be to Kentucky what Oberlin is to Ohio, and an antislavery, anti-caste, anti-tobacco, anti-sectarian school . . . a school under Christian influence; a school that will furnish the best possible facilities for those of small means who have energy of character that will lead them to work their way through this world. . . . The place for the college is here in the interior of Kentucky.

Berea College, in Berea, Kentucky, was opened in 1859. After considerable debate as to whether "colored children should be admitted into the school room with white children," two boards of directors—one proslavery, the other antislavery— were placed in nomination. The antislavery directors won by a better than two-to-one majority. The Rev. John A.R. Rogers was chosen first principal of the school. Mr. Rogers announced that he would not accept appointment as principal unless the school would be open to everyone. But all was not well. In 1860 a proslavery public meeting was held in Richmond, Kentucky, the county seat. Sixty-two persons were appointed to go to Berea to warn the teachers that they must leave within ten days. This was the beginning of the expulsion of all missionaries and the closing of all missions in Kentucky and in North Carolina. Then came the Civil War, and Berea College did not reopen until 1865. Three Negro students applied for admission, and for the first time in the South, Negroes were admitted to a school on equal basis with white students. Many whites withdrew but some later returned to school.

The slaveholders were not quiet during this period. In politics, in Congress, in state legislatures, and even in churches, every available means of resistance and protest was resorted to, including violence or threat of violence. Once when John Fee went to keep an appointment with a young lawyer for a discussion on the question of slavery, instead of the receptive audience he expected, he found a lawless mob of about forty profane men, who insisted that there would be no discussion and who demanded that he should not preach there again and that he should leave the house. When he declined to go, he was taken by force, put upon his horse, and with the help of sticks the horse was started on its way. All the while the crowd indulged in vulgar abuse and in threats of violence. On a later occasion another mob came into the church while Fee was preaching and demanded that he stop and remain silent in the future. When he openly refused, he was forced to take off part of his clothing. This he did, and he knelt to receive the lashes from the whips. For some strange reason the lashes never came, and the mob left him kneeling and waiting.

The issue of slavery brought division in churches. Baptists, Methodists, and Presbyterians became Northern- or Southern-. Congregationalists did not split, probably because there were no Congregational churches in the South. North and south, ministers and other churchpeople, as well as politicians, expressed their views boldly, often with hate and bitterness. Both sides used the Bible to support their positions. Many, both north and south, kept quiet to avoid involvement. Several recorded items and quotations may help to clarify the nature and the extent of the struggle. In his message to Congress, in December 1835, President Jackson, with abolitionist literature in mind, recommended the passage of a law that would prohibit circulation through the mails of any "incendiary publications." Two months later Sen. John C. Calhoun, of South Carolina, introduced a bill that required Congress to prohibit the circulation of a publication that had been declared incendiary by a state. Congress defeated this bill but passed a gag rule that was at least as conciliatory, in that it provided that "all petitions relating in any way to slavery be laid on the table without being printed or referred." This rule was maintained in the Congress for several years.

Elijah P. Lovejoy, an abolitionist, was a staunch crusader. A champion of the right of free speech, he was editor of *The Observer*, which was regarded as incendiary because it spoke out against slavery. As a result of being persecuted, Lovejoy moved from St. Louis to Alton, Illinois, a free state. But here too he was mobbed; rocks were hurled through the windows of his place of business and his home, and his printing press was destroyed. He secured a new press and continued publication. Mob violence was renewed. Lovejoy was shot and killed one night, after he and a group of his friends armed themselves for defense against the mob.

Calhoun was scheduled to give a prepared speech in Congress on March 4, 1850, but became very sick with tuberculosis. The speech, which was read by his close friend, Sen. James Mason, of Virginia, stated that the North "must cease all agitation against slavery, return the fugitive slaves willingly, and restore to the South her equal rights in all parts of the Union and all acquired territory. Otherwise the cords which had bound the states together for two generations would every one be broken, and our Republic would be dissolved into warring factions." These were Calhoun's last public words. He died later that month. Many of Calhoun's demands became part of the laws that made up the Compromise of 1850.

Bishop Mead, of the Protestant Episcopal Church, gave this advice to slaves:

Almighty God has been pleased to make you slaves . . . which you are obliged to submit to, as it is His will that it be so. . . . A general rule that you ought to always carry in your minds is to do all service (for your masters) as if you did it for God Himself. . . . Do what your masters under God provide for you to do. . . . Take care that you do not fret or murmur or grumble at your condition, for this not only makes your life miserable, but will greatly offend Almighty God. . . . When correction is given you . . . whether you deserve it or not, it is your duty, and Almighty God requires that you bear it patiently.

A church resolution adopted in Clinton, Mississippi read:

Resolved, that in our decided opinion that any individual who dares to circulate, with a view to effectuate the designs of the abolitionists and of the incendiary tracts of newspapers now in course of transmission to this country, is justly worthy, in the sight of man and God, of immediate death; and we doubt not that such would be the punishment of any such offender in any part of the State of Mississippi where he may be found.

Similar feelings found expression in all southern states.

Attitudes in the North varied. Opposition to slavery grew, although some northern partisans tried desperately to prevent the expression of opinions regarding it. Most northern churches were silent. Even though they may have regarded slavery as morally evil, they respected the rights of independent states and were influenced by southern racial bias. For instance, in New Haven, Connecticut, persons of color were excluded from white schools. The Connecticut legislature, after much discussion, passed a law that made it a crime to teach any colored child from another state. This law was occasioned when Prudence Crandall opened a school for colored girls only in Canterbury, Connecticut. She was persecuted and brought into court under the new law. After being convicted in the lower courts, she appealed to the Supreme Court of Errors and finally won her case.

However, much can be said for some of those who opposed slavery and for some acts of the Congress and of state legislatures. When a series of Gag Rules was adopted by Congress in 1836, John Quincy Adams stated: "I hold the resolution to be a direct violation of the Constitution of the United States, of the rules of this House, and of the rights of my constituents." The Connecticut law referred to was declared unconstitutional by its own Supreme Court of Errors. On the violent side, the story of John Brown is a matter of history. Brown believed fanatically that he was divinely guided to free the slaves. He avowed that "twenty men in the Alleghenies could break slavery to pieces in two years." His scheme was to set up small groups of armed men in the Appalachian Mountains who would raid the plains at night and kidnap slaves and take them to these "camps of freedom." On October 16, 1859, with a group of twenty-one followers that included three of his sons and five Negroes, Brown seized the U.S. arsenal at Harpers Ferry, Virginia, raided a few nearby plantations, and forcibly freed about thirty slaves. Shortly thereafter, on October 18, a detachment of U.S. Marines under the command of Col. Robert E. Lee captured John Brown. While in prison Brown stated that it was not his design to commit murder, to destroy property, or to excite slaves to rebellion but only "to free the Slaves." His only defense at his trial was a claim of divine commission. He was speedily convicted and hanged. To the proslavery South he was a dangerous criminal, guilty of insurrection and treason. To most of the antislavery North he was a martyr, and "he became a sort of patron saint to the Northern armies during the Civil War."

Before the American Missionary Association was formed, several smaller missionary groups with strong antislavery sentiments were at work. One of the oldest of these was the Amistad Committee, initially composed of the Rev. Simeon S. Jocelyn, the Rev. Joshua Leavitt, and Lewis Tappan. This committee volunteered to provide religious instruction and legal defense for the forty-four survivors out of fifty-three Africans who had been kidnapped, brought to Cuba, and sold to Cuban slaveholders for a sum of $450 each. The Africans had been loaded on *La Amistad*, a small Spanish slave schooner, to be taken to another Cuban port. When told by the cook that they were to be killed and eaten, they mutinied, captured the ship, and tried to sail back to Africa. This attempt was aborted, and they finally cast anchor on the northern coast of Long Island. The Africans were confined in several locations, and technically they were prisoners for only a short time. During this period they were tried in the federal courts of Connecticut and finally appealed to the Supreme Court of the United States. Roger S. Baldwin and John Quincy Adams provided legal counsel for the defense. Finally, the Africans were "declared free to be dismissed from the custody of the court and to go without delay." After they were released, Baldwin remarked that "their freedom was a barren gift," for they were here "in a state where they might be pitied but were not wanted, and were separated from their homes by the distance of half the globe." The Amistad Committee, its funds largely supplemented by Arthur Tappan, took responsibility for returning the men to Africa and for establishing the Mendi Mission.

By 1854 the American Missionary Association had missionaries at stations in Africa, Jamaica, the Hawaiian Islands, Siam, Egypt, as well as among American Indians and Negro fugitives who had found a refuge in Canada. At the same time it entered heartily into the work of upbuilding antislavery churches at home, employing by 1860, 112 home missionaries, chiefly in Ohio, Indiana, Michigan, Illinois, Wisconsin, Minnesota, Iowa and Kansas. A few of its missionaries were laboring among the whites of the slaves states, especially in Kentucky and . . . in North Carolina, encountering everywhere much popular opposition.

As long as slavery existed, the Negro population of the South was beyond any appreciable effects of the work of the association. As the Civil War approached, the intensity of the persecution and the violence increased. All missions in the South were closed, and missionaries were forced to leave the area.

The bombardment of Fort Sumter, in Charleston harbor, South Carolina, April 12, 1861 signaled the beginning of the Civil War. It also marked an increase in personal sacrifice and danger of physical violence for missionaries or for others who in any way gave assistance to runaway slaves or Freedmen.

During the war years the association never lacked for volunteers, both men and women, who were eager to serve as missionaries, in the cause of freedom. Work continued in the "West, from Ohio to Kansas." Association missionaries followed the Union armies into the South. The first school for Freedmen was opened at Hampton, Virginia on September 17, 1861, and as the war continued, schools were started in Norfolk, Virginia; Washington, D.C.; New Bern, North Carolina, and in many other places where occupation had been achieved by the Union armies. The urgent imperative of the mission was fourfold:—to Christianize and elevate the morals of liberated slaves; to teach the simple rudiments of education, reading, writing, and arithmetic, to adults and to children; to provide the simple necessities of life such as food, clothing, shelter; and to encourage acceptable habits of personal cleanliness and social conduct.

The following quotations from reports and letters published in the *American Missionary* and from minutes of the annual meetings of the American Missionary Association will better tell the story of the dangers and hardships endured by the missionaries and of the destitute conditions of the Freedmen.

AN APPEAL FOR THE FREEDMEN (Prepared by a Committee appointed at the Annual meeting of the American Missionary Association, October 16, 1862)

In the Providence of God, tens of thousands of freed slaves are now waiting in various parts of the South for the privileges which freedom confers and slavery has denied them. The number is constantly increasing, and within a few months it is probable that hundreds of thousands will be looking to their friends for aid, and what class of people ever presented a better claim to charity! Indeed, it hardly deserves the name of charity to supply their wants. They only ask a little interest and a long time debt.

[1.] Their first wants are physical. They have escaped from bondage in a very destitute condition. They need clothes, bedding, and some shelter from the storm.

[2.] They need education. Few of them can read or write. They need day schools and night schools for children and adults. Every family should at once be supplied with the Bible.

[3.] They need the preaching of the Gospel. . . .

[4.] They need assistance in organizing themselves into schools, Sabbath schools, congregations and churches; and they need intelligent friends and counselors to guard them against the insults, impositions, immoralities and various abuses of those who hate them, and are determined to prove that Negroes are an improvident race. . . .

To all Christian ministers we make our appeal, urging them to bring the matter before their respective congregations immediately, and take up collections for the object. . . .

To every benevolent individual we say, do not fail to have a share in this most important and most promising work. Send money, boxes of clothing and bedding to Lewis Tappan, Esq., Treasurer, 61 John Street, New York. . . .

There was also an appeal made to ministers and teachers who were "able and willing to enter this field of labor" to come forward and offer their services to the American Missionary Association.

From a letter dated November 21, 1862, from a woman in Johnson County, Kansas (name withheld for safety reasons):

I write to enclose to you one dollar for your society. I wish I could send a hundred times as much, for I have felt very solicitous for the poor "contrabands," and have wished them near me, to benefit them. (None nearer us than Wyandotte or Lawrence—20 or 30 miles away.)

When Quantrille visited our town September 6, several of our worthy citizens were shot without any provocation. Three were taken from their homes and beds to the prairie and shot. Since Quantrille visited our town, he has visited several other places and committed like barbarities. At Shawnee town they burned 14 houses, destroyed a vast amount of property, and killed three men in town and three at the spring four miles from town.

From a report from the Rev. L.C. Lockwood, who was in charge of the mission at Fort Monroe, near Hampton, Virginia—1862:

We were kindly received by General Wood who was in command there, and have received from him encouragement in our mission. . . .

Most of them have resided in Hampton, left there on its evacuation by our troops, and lost nearly all of their clothing and other effects; they were reduced to great destitution. . . . The people, many of them, were religious, belonged to the Baptist Church in Hampton, which at one time, was composed of about eight hundred colored persons and two hundred whites. We arranged at once for preaching and other services at three points: the Fortress, the Seminary, and the Tyler House, the former residence of John Tyler, ex-President of the United States, near Hampton.

Sabbath schools were established at these points. . . . The teacher was a devoted colored woman, Mrs. Peake, whose intelligence and virtue won for her universal respect, and whose labors were connected with excellent results. She [Mrs. Peake] died on the 22nd of February, 1862, sleeping sweetly in Jesus.

The day school at the Fortress was for a time taught by colored persons, and afterwards by white teachers. The evidence of the aptitude of the children to learn, and the desire of the adults for knowledge were strikingly manifest. Elementary books and all the materials for instruction were provided, and the work went forward with cheering results.

While American Missionary Association reports show that Virginia was the scene of the first missions among Freedmen in the South, that "here was the first school for ex-slaves, and here during the year (1864–65) the largest number of our missionaries and teachers, and here the most extended results" were realized, according to the report, no Congregational church for Negroes was organized in Virginia. This seems strange, for at almost no other point in the South where the association established schools for Negroes did it fail to establish Congregational churches and sabbath schools. There are now thirty-two Black Christian churches (Congregational Christian—United Church of Christ) in the Tidewater and in adjacent areas of Virginia, the same areas in which the American Missionary Association first established its ministry. One can only speculate as to what influence mission schools may have had upon the very versatile, alert, and dedicated Black ministers and lay leaders of the first Black Christian churches in Virginia. It is only speculation, but it is very fascinating speculation.

Friday, April 14, 1865, was the fourth anniversary of the

surrender of Fort Sumter to Confederate forces. On that day a great celebration took place at Charleston, South Carolina, and Gen. Robert Anderson raised above Fort Sumter the same ragged flag he had hauled down after the bombardment, in 1861. Here, at Fort Sumter, the shooting war began; here the shooting war ended. But the conflict was far from being settled. Hate had been engendered; the whole nation, particularly the South, had been impoverished; thousands of the bravest and best of North and South lay dead upon battlefields and in the swamps and marshes of Virginia, the Carolinas, Georgia, Mississippi. The North was greedy to possess and control the South, and the poor, bewildered Black, still a slave to poverty and ignorance, was caught in the middle of this, our worst national conflict.

It was out of this great national travail that Negro churches and Negro denominations were born; Black Congregational churches of the South can date their beginning from about 1865. Let it be remembered, however, that there were dedicated white ministers who came to the rescue when there was need for guidance and counsel in the intricate matters of church organization and polity. No group of churches in the South is more aware and appreciative of this fact than Black Congregational churches.

Chapter 3

Beginnings and Early Development
of Black Congregational Churches
in the South

Black Congregational churches in the South were the off-spring of the home missionary work of the American Missionary Association. The earliest of these churches were organized by white Congregational ministers who came south as missionary teachers to work in schools and colleges that had been started by the American Missionary Association. These churches were frequently referred to as AMA churches. They were an essential development of the mission of the association, for the association worked with Indians, mountain whites, and other undeveloped minorities in America, especially in the South, and not only with Freedmen.

By the time the guns of the War Between the States were silenced, the American Missionary Association was already at work. Commissioned workers followed the Union forces along the Atlantic coast, from Virginia to Florida, down the Ohio and the Mississippi rivers and the Gulf coast. Thousands of Black Freedmen and slaves escaped to Union camps—men, women, and children in need of food, clothing, shelter, and protection from their desperate and enraged slavemasters—many with nothing more than the clothes they wore. Such slaves were declared "contrabands of war" by Gen. Benjamin Franklin Butler; gradually this designation became common. Missionaries came into the Union camps as teachers and religious workers. Housing for contrabands, teachers, schools, and religious services were provided in captured homes or buildings and in army barracks.

The first American Missionary Association school in the South for colored people was opened at Fort Monroe, near Hampton, Virginia, September 17, 1861. A teacher who had been commissioned by the association wrote from Fort Monroe:

There are 1,800 contrabands here; yesterday I opened a Sabbath-school in Ex-President Tyler's mansion. Little did he think it would ever be used for such a purpose. Parents and children are delighted with the idea of learning to read. All felt that it was the beginning of better days for them and for their children.

This first day school for Freedmen began with an enrollment of twenty pupils. Within a week the enrollment grew to about fifty pupils. Mary Peake was the first teacher. Although she was light in complexion, she identified with the Blacks. The Rev. C.L. Lockwood helped her by securing from the government a cottage that could be used for a classroom and that also had living quarters above. Here she lived the remainder of her life, teaching fifty children every morning and a large class of adults every afternoon. Lockwood described her and her work in glowing terms:

Mrs. Peake is a free woman, quite light colored, with qualifications for the post. She is devotedly pious and highly respected by her own people in the community. She will make a good permanent teacher worthy of compensation. Mrs. Peake had made the most of her chance for education in the District of Columbia before the schools there were closed to her race; and in slavery times, and at great personal risk, had taught, not only her husband, but scores of Negroes who had come to her cabin by night to learn to read.

Mary Peake, a native of Norfolk, Virginia, was born in the year 1823. Already in declining health when she opened the day school, she never knew that this pioneer school was destined to become the world famous Hampton Normal and Agricultural Institute. In the room above the school she died on Saturday, February 22, 1862. Soon the American Missionary Association sent other teachers. A burned-out courthouse in Hampton, after being repaired, became the new location for the school. The move was made in October 1862, with an enrollment of over 300 pupils.

After the momentous Emancipation Proclamation was issued, on January 1, 1863, the compelling cry was education for the former slaves. None responded to this cry with so great devotion and dedication as did the American Missionary Association. Schools were opened in Newport News, Norfolk, Portsmouth, Suffolk, and Yorktown, Virginia. (It is interesting to note that although Virginia is the only state of the Confederate South where Congregational schools were started, no Congregational churches were organized among the Blacks.) The records indicate a genuine religious fervor in all schools of the association, as well as considerable evangelistic effort in the Sunday schools and in the day schools. In Virginia, however, converts were directed to existing churches of the area. Later, in tidewater Virginia, about forty-five Black Christian churches were organized, thirty-two of which are still in existence. Any attempt to trace the influence of the association schools, except Hampton and possibly Yorktown (Capahosic), to any Black Christian churches in eastern Virginia has been fruitless.

In 1862 the second school in the South for Black people was opened at Hilton Head, South Carolina. Teachers sent from Boston by the association included three Yale graduates. These teachers pioneered in opening schools at Beaufort, St. Helena, and Port Royal, all on the sea islands of South Carolina. From 1863 association missionaries followed the paths of victorious Union forces and planted mission schools for Blacks along the Mississippi River and its tributaries at Memphis and Nashville in Tennessee, at Vicksburg and Natchez in Mississippi, at Helena and Little Rock in Arkansas, and at New Orleans and Port Hudson in Louisiana. They followed General Sherman's trail of march across Georgia, and schools were started in Atlanta, Macon, Milledgeville, McIntosh, and Savannah. Along the coasts, schools were started at Beaufort, New Bern, and Wilmington, North Carolina; Charleston, South Carolina; Jacksonville, Florida; Mobile, Alabama; and Corpus Christi, Texas. Within five years after the close of the Civil War there were over 300 mission schools for Blacks, some in each of the Confederate states and also in Missouri, in Maryland, and in the District of Columbia.

Hundreds of missionaries worked in these schools. The majority were women, because women could remain where men would not be tolerated by an angry South. Yet many of these women were ostracized by the white South and suffered numerous indignities at the hands of the Ku-Klux Klan. Schools were broken into, and some teachers were forced to leave their posts of service. In Austin, Texas the post commander sent a guard to escort the teacher to and from her school and to stand by during the day. In Athens, Alabama the Klan lined up outside the schoolroom and fired shots through the window at both sides of the chair where the teacher was sitting, but she did not run. Instead, she remained at Athens for twenty years and developed a successful normal school in which many northern Alabama teachers were trained.

The aristocracy of the South came out of the Civil War defeated and doubly impoverished. Lands had been confiscated; slaves, who constituted a considerable portion of the South's wealth, had been declared free. Most of the war's destruction was visited upon the South. Many fine homes were seized, ransacked, or destroyed. Food animals and poultry and food crops were fed to the invading armies and to the "contrabands" who escaped to the Union camps. Even some agents of the Freedmen's Bureau took advantage of the helplessness of the whites and of the gross ignorance of the Blacks to enlarge their own gain. Southerners were humiliated and enraged. The Blacks and those who assumed responsibility for their religious and literary training were victims of this anger. Night riders and Klan-groups were organized and soon spread rapidly across the South. Wherever there were schools or churches for Blacks or residential concentrations of Blacks, the mask and the hood were familiar and frightful nightmares. Those who wore them stopped at nothing to revenge their defeat and to regain southern white supremacy. There were senseless beatings, killings, and lynchings; churches and schools were burned; and a white person was seldom, if ever, held for any crime against a Black person.

Names of missionaries and teachers who reported any of the barbaric crimes were rarely given, but their reports appeared monthly in the *American Missionary*. The press, both North and South, carried articles describing some of these crimes. The *Memphis* (Tennessee) *Post* reported that

two whites and a Negro residing near Holly Springs, Mississippi, were recently returning from Memphis. They stopped for dinner at a bridge on Cold Water Creek, when the white men ordered the Negro to bring them some water. While he was stooping down to dip up some water, they fired upon him, but not so seriously as to prevent his getting into the woods and making his way to some neighbors, to whom he told his tale, the facts of which have since been corroborated. The Negro is still living, and has endeavored to obtain a warrant for the arrest of the men who fired upon him, but had not succeeded at last accounts. The white men are his near neighbors, and belong to the chivalry of that section of the country. They claim to have *fired upon the Negro in sport as a mere matter of pastime.*

The *New York Tribune* carried the following news item:

A mysterious occurrence took place here about ten days ago [Coffeeville, Mississippi] that has not yet been unraveled, and it is probable that it never will be. There lived here a Freedman, who was a preacher and a school teacher. He taught here in the Spring and had about 20 scholars, but did not have more than four or five months. . . . A few nights ago, just after dark, someone rode up to where the preacher stayed, called him out and told him that someone wanted to see him "down there a little ways." Directly two gun shots were heard a short distance away. . . . Two days after this the corpse of the preacher was found with a ball-hole through the head, and another through his side.

On September 20, 1866 *The Loyal Georgian,* Augusta, Georgia, gave the following account:

Mount Zion Church, owned by the colored people of Beach Island, Edgecomb District, S.C., was destroyed by fire on Saturday night, the 8th of September. As usual, the fire was the work of a white "friend." . . . The church was built upon land given to them several years ago by a benevolent white gentleman, now deceased, but his son refuses to let them retain it, as they have no deed for it, and also refuses to sell it, as he and his white neighbors "have got tired of free niggers having church" in their neighborhood. . . .

Laurence Gardner has been driven from his home in Hancock County, because he exercised the indefensable right as a Freedman of meeting with his brethren from other counties in a Convention in this city in July last. A mob had collected to dispose of him upon his return from the Convention; but a delay in his return, and timely warning from his friends, saved him.

Many reports such as these appeared frequently in news journals of the South. But there were also excellent reports on the other side of the ledger. From Dudley, North Carolina, Pastor John Scott reported:

> The work of the Association at this point has been unique. . . . A tract of seven hundred acres of land was purchased at Dudley and divided into ten- and twenty-acre lots; and then plundered and fleeing families were invited to come and put up their cabins, and pay the first cost of their patches as they could raise the money. In the colony, and for the other colored people around, a school was opened, and, through the assistance of the Bureau, a commodious and, for that county, a fine school-house had been erected, which furnished a convenient chapel for the Sabbath services. . . . .
>
> The better part of the colored people were found desirous of a church organization. For some miles around, there was no church of any kind for this large colored population. Out of this material twelve members and three young converts were united in a church of Christ. At the organization, the church asked for the ordination of their teacher, Mr. John Scott, to the ministry of the Gospel among them. . . . While it will not, in that wretched county, hold any marked place in the church work of North Carolina, it will be a light and comfort and salvation to many poor, struggling families around. The present membership is 35 [fall of 1870]. The Sabbath-school numbers 100.

In February 1871 this "fine school-house" was set afire by arsonists, who were never apprehended; but,

> pursuant to a call, a large meeting of the citizens of Brogden Township, Wayne County (Irrespective of color) was held at Dudley on Saturday, February 25, to express the indignation and condemnation of the good citizens at the lawless act—the burning of the colored people's school-house, near Dudley, on the night of Monday, February 20, 1871.

At that meeting a reward of $100 was posted for the arrest of the person (or persons) guilty of setting the fire. Also on that occasion the township citizens raised over $500 in cash and pledged timber and whatever assistance they could give toward the erection of a new schoolhouse. The whites also offered the free use of their church building by the colored school and church until "such time as their own new building would be ready for use." With the cooperation of the whole community the new building was ready by October 1871. (When I went to Dudley in 1931 this building still stood as a landmark, furnished with desks and pews made on the site, and served as the leading place of worship in this community. On several occasions the public schools of Wayne County had requested the use of this building and, in return, had allowed the Dudley school building to be used for church services while the present church was being erected. The most lasting timbers in the foundation and structure of the present building were salvaged from the schoolhouse chapel that the Rev. John Scott and his friends built at Dudley in 1871.)

In 1871 the governor of Georgia became acutely concerned because of rumors of the liberal training that was being given to colored people at Atlanta University. He appointed a nine-member board of visitors and issued instructions to visit the institution and to report the findings to him. The board of visitors gave the following report:

Atlanta, Georgia
June 28, 1871
To His Excellency R.B. Bullock,
Governor of Georgia:

The Board of Visitors appointed by your excellency to attend the examination of the students of the "Normal and Preparatory Departments of the Atlanta University," on the 26th and 27th Inst., have the honor to report that the undersigned have performed the duty assigned to them, having given earnest attention to all the examination exercises on the days designated in your order of appointment.

The Atlanta University was incorporated in the year 1867, and has now been in active operation about two years. Designed to afford opportunity for thorough education to members of a race only recently elevated to citizenship, and much of its prescribed curriculum of studies being of a higher grade than that of other institutions in the South whose doors are open to pupils of color, it is, in our section of the country, a novel enterprise, concerning the success and usefulness of which much interest is felt all over the Union.

We therefore deem it our duty, not only to give the examination the strictest attention, but also to carefully scrutinize every thing pertaining to the management of the institution.

The examination was conducted fairly and truly indicative of the character of the mental training to which the students have been subjected, and the attainments of each in his or her studies.

We were agreeably impressed with the numerous evidences of the patience, painstaking perseverance, and professional skill of the teachers, which the thorough training and admirable demeanor of the pupils demonstrated. . . . The progress of their classes and the thoroughness of their teaching, and the unmistakable evidences visible on every hand of order, system, and judicious discipline, have won this testimony from us.

The exercises of the examination were conducted strictly in the order indicated in the printed programme, a copy of which is herewith transmitted.

At every step of the examination we were impressed with the fallacy of the popular idea (which, in common with thousands of others, a majority of the undersigned have heretofore entertained) that members of the African race are not capable of a high grade of intellectual culture. . . . Many of the pupils exhibited a degree of mental culture which, considering the length of time their minds have been in training, would do credit to members of any race. We fully satisfied ourselves that the system of intellectual and moral training adopted in the institution is eminently practical.

We are convinced that the funds placed in the hands of the managers have been wisely expended. That so much good has been done with the means at command has been chiefly due to the missionary spirit with which the teachers . . . have performed their arduous duties, while receiving salaries barely sufficient to supply the necessaries of life. . . .

We heartily commend the institution to the fostering care of the State, whose appropriation in aid of it, we are satisfied, has thus far been judiciously expended, to the attention of benevolently inclined throughout the country, and to the kindly sympathy and approval of the people in whose midst it is located. . . .

In discharging the duty to which we were assigned by your Excellency, for consideration not necessary to recount, we have felt that it was our duty to give to you, and through you to the public, a report strictly according to the facts. Of the justice of this report, the incredulous can satisfy themselves by visiting the institution, as we have done, with an eye single to the truth.

Very respectfully yours,

Joseph E. Brown,   Jared Irwin Whitaker,
John L. Hopkins,   William L. Scruggs,
James L. Dunning,   D. Mayer,
W. A. Hemphill,   S. H. Stout.
John H. Knowles,

From a teacher who visited "at Marion, Alabama a short time" came this report:

The most interesting prayer-meeting that I ever attended among the Freedmen was in Alabama, in the Ku-Klux region, where they at the "Mission Home" looked well to their guns and their rifles before retiring. I reached there on Wednesday night, the evening of the weekly prayer-meeting in the school house. 'Twas a stormy night, but with water-proofs and umbrellas we ventured. Wholly unused to bullets, I must confess, there was a little trembling under *one* water-proof, as we wended our way along the little path through the woods, and across the plank bridge over the "Branch." But once within the building, all fear vanished. The room was filled with the finest looking colored people I ever saw. . . .

The pastor [George W. Andrews, of Talladega College]

an able and ready man . . . opened the meeting, and then gave it into the hands of the colored brethren, and they carried it on with a liveliness that was truly refreshing.

They had no church building, and had been striving hard to get ready to build, . . . but even at that time they faced the danger of their being obliged to disband, for outside violence was not entirely over. But as they told of their love for their church, I could hardly help thinking of those stories we all read in our childhood, of Christians in early days, when persecutions but increased their zeal. . . . And then one after another they kneeled down, and, in the most simple words of faith, asked their Father to help His children in their day of Special trouble. . . .

At a meeting just before the close of the term [1870–71] as I learned from a teacher, one after another rose and pledged himself to do a certain amount toward erecting the building during the Summer.

Despite numerous instances of tortures, burnings, and killings, there were signs of hope in every state of the old Confederacy. Anger and hostility toward northern white missionaries who worked among the colored people mellowed; southern banks and merchants began to welcome the patronage of the schools and colleges; and all of the southern states began to provide at least token education for Blacks, although at the higher levels most states insisted upon *industrial* education as a means of "keeping the Negro in his place." But these attitudes were only incipient in those early years. Black folk and their missionary benefactors suffered untold hardships, persecutions, and, frequently, organized violent treatment from the white citizenry of the South.

The story of one missionary teacher illustrates the fortitude of many others:

In McLeansville (Sedalia), North Carolina, Esther W. Douglass opened a school for Blacks in an old Confederate gun factory. One white man offered to be one of a group to put her on the train, by force if necessary, and send her away. She bravely retorted, "I was sent by the American Missionary Association, and when they say 'Go,' I will, and not before." She did not go. Her school and church work at McLeansville, Sedalia, and

Wadsworth (Whitsett) and at Oaks, Cedar Cliff, and Melville, all in North Carolina, is beautifully described in her diary and in letters to the American Missionary Association and to other friends.

Esther Douglass gives excellent testimony to the sacrifice, the dedication, and the untiring patience and work, under trying circumstances, of these teachers and ministers of the association. Her work with the association began in 1865 at the government lumber camp situated in the "grand forests" between Hampton and Newport News, Virginia. From there she wrote:

Our government had two steam mills sawing lumber for army uses. The only people there were the few white families whose men worked in the mills and the families of refugees who had come into our lines, whose men were cutting down the trees and hauling logs to the mills. . . . I drew rations like the soldiers—pork every day, coffee, sugar and bread or flour. I sold or gave away my meat and coffee and bought eggs or whatever I pleased. . . . There was no minister except when the Chaplain came from Hampton for a day to marry any who were ready to be married.

My School was very pleasant, only there were some white children and their parents thought they ought to have special favors. On the Sabbath I was busy teaching all the day—meeting morning, afternoon and evening, and between these hours, teaching the men to read. . . . When work at the mills was given up I went North to friends in Vermont. In the fall I was commissioned to Ogeechee, Georgia.

About Ogeechee (Savannah), Georgia, Esther Douglass wrote:

We went out from Savannah in an ambulance. All the way we saw the fruits of war—bones of cattle and horses, twisted rails and a broken engine. Words can give you no idea of the utter destitution of these ex-slaves. . . . With the obstacles in the way of these colored people, I often wondered that so many of them had the courage to try to be anything respectable.

Northern men who hired the land before the owners were pardoned did not care for the good of the people, but only to make as much as possible out of their labor—at least those I knew on seven plantations, and some men of the Freedmen's Bureau were no better.

There was with me a young woman and we had two rooms upstairs [in the ruined mansion house of the H. Plantation]. Mr. H. had had a little Church and an Episcopal minister for his slaves. Miss Littlefield taught in the church and I in the Mansion house parlor. Think of 120 black, half naked, dirty, perfectly wild children crowded together on the floor and you will have some idea of my task the first morning of my school. Finally, I made them understand that the bell meant silence and they were to repeat after me as I pointed to words on the card on the wall. Their progress was wonderful. Before we went home in June '66 they had learned to read and spell all on the cards. There were words of five syllables, and verses that they learned to sing. They had learned much of God's truth [from the Bible] and had stopped fighting. At first those of different plantations, each claiming their "folks as the grandest," fought like cats and dogs.

At the close of the summer vacation of 1866, both women returned to the H. plantation "and were joyfully welcomed by our colored friends." Their former students brought them gifts of peanuts, eggs, rice, and sweet potatoes. "But Col. Waddell said he wanted all the mission house; and we had no where to live, so the rejoicing was turned to mourning." After fruitless attempts to reestablish their school at a nearby plantation and at Grove Hill, also in Chatham County, Georgia,

there was a call for teachers on Donifuskie Island, and we went there, and so I soon found myself in the Palmetto State [South Carolina]. . . . We came from Savannah 20 miles by row boat, landing at Bloody Point, three miles from the plantation where we were to live.

The fine mansion house had escaped injury. . . . The garden was a world of beauty. Mr. Stoddard, the owner, gave Mr. Pettibone leave to take from other houses and enclose the large boat house and fit it for our use.

Here they worked for the remainder of the school year. With a cooling sea breeze, the teachers decided to
work on through the summer, and went to Savannah to get

supplies. Miss Littlefield was seized with Billious fever and the doctor said she must go North. I went back to the Island, taking a barrel of supplies, expecting that when the schools closed in Savannah, a teacher would come to be with me. Before the boat reached the Island, I was too sick to sit up and knew I had the fever.

For three weeks I was on my bed there before the teacher came. . . . Colored women came in to do my bidding there and brought oysters and chicken but I could not eat. They had to go to the field to work but children stayed within call. . . . I tried to get well after the teacher came, but in vain, so one day my bed was laid on the boat and I on it. The house was shut and to Savannah we went. From the boat I was taken to a berth in a steamer bound for New York. . . . By the time we reached New York I was able to sit up and ride to a hotel. In a few days I was able to go to friends in Vermont. My sister and her husband were Missionaries in Nashville, Tennessee, and when I was stronger, I went to them.

The next work Esther Douglass had was at Union Hill, near Lebanon, Tennessee. An "old bachelor minister" who had been turned out of the Methodist church because he was loyal to the Union had built his own church in which he preached to his people. He applied to the mission in Nashville for a teacher and she had accepted the call.

I was told that nothing but a Methodist would suit him, and thought I would like to teach him better, so I went. . . . Mr. Seay did everything he could for my comfort, and had me send for Miss Frances Littlefield for company. He was one of the great preachers before the war, but now none of his friends or relatives would have anything to do with him. . . . He kept a loaded gun and two pistols by his bed, and every window in the house was closed at night by heavy wooden shutters, securely fastened. Jack, a very large Black man, Tennersee's husband, was to guard me, at home at night, and to and from school and church each morning and evening.

For two years Esther Douglass taught at Union Hill, but when one of the teachers at Nashville became ill, she was sent there (Fisk University). In addition to teaching, she visited regularly at the hospital for colored people and also went to the penitentiary with other teachers every Sunday and taught a Sunday school class of fourteen men. In her diary she wrote: "I was glad when the teacher recovered, for city children were not as good as those in the country, and I liked my other work better."

In 1871 the American Missionary Association sent Esther Douglass to McLeansville (Alamance), North Carolina. Two years earlier the Rev. John Scott, missionary teacher at Dudley, North Carolina, came to McLeansville and was instrumental in organizing three Congregational churches—First (McLeansville), Bethany (Sedalia), and Wadsworth (Whitsett). Scott's services were offered part-time, for he also served newly organized churches at Dudley and at Beaufort, North Carolina. Douglass taught Black children during the day and instructed classes for adults at night in the remains of a Confederate gun factory. During her first year a white family, Mr. and Mrs. Clapp, offered her room and board if she would teach their children after school hours. While she was there, however, none of the Clapps' friends, except one of Mr. Clapp's sisters, came to visit them. When Esther Douglass arrived at McLeansville, no one was there to meet her. She hired the station man to take her the three miles to the Clapp home. "Along the way, I was entertained by my driver's stories of the KKK's doings as we passed the places where there had been whippings and hangings. I ventured to ask if it would not be better to punish crime lawfully. The answer was 'No nigger ever gets more than he deserved.'"

Esther Douglass remained in this area for several years. A major part of her work was with the churches, where she helped with their organization, taught in the Sabbath schools, and regularly attended preaching services, prayer meetings, and other meetings. During her stay each of the three churches got its first building, one of which (Sedalia) had rooms at one end for her. She stayed for several years in the teaching ministry, cementing lasting friendship among the Black people and softening many of the whites' attitude toward her.

In 1880 she was sent by the association to Liberty County, Georgia, which was only a few miles from where she began work in 1865. She was missionary at three stations—Miller's Station, Golding's Grove, and Cypress Slash. There was a minister-teacher at each of these stations, "all colored." The minister at Miller's Station, the Rev. John Rufus McLean, a native of McLeansville, North Carolina, was one of Esther Douglass' first pupils there. In 1881, after four years at Miller's Station, McLean was encouraged to enter Talladega College, from which he graduated in 1884. After graduation he served Congregational churches in Georgia, in Texas, and in Alabama. His last pastorate was at First Congregational Church, Greensboro, North Carolina. He died April 7, 1919 in Greensboro, only a few miles from his place of birth.

Using Miller's Station as home base, Esther Douglass spent a month at a time at each of these stations, working with the preacher and the church people and teaching Bible classes and Sunday school. Frequently, she traveled at night by horse and buggy to outstations to teach the Bible and to teach the adults to read and write. She visited the oldest Congregational church in the South, at Midway, Georgia, and "had a Bible Reading in it with a large company of colored people." In Liberty County much of the land was owned or bargained for by Blacks. She describes the people as being very industrious; nearly all were church members, although they had never learned the lesson of forgiveness "but believed in conjuring their enemies. . . . Every where I went I found the people believing in silly superstitions."

Before the end of her second year in Liberty County, there was sickness in the mission home in Savannah, and she was called there to take the place of a sick teacher.

When [the teacher] recovered, I was retained as a City Missionary. I enjoyed that very much.

As I went through street after street I found many comfortable homes occupied by colored people. I think the dirtiest place I saw was occupied by three white sisters. One of them was a fortune teller. One of them seemed interested when I talked and read to them, but they were very ignorant. . . . When [the other teachers] went North for the Summer vacation, a colored woman and I were left to keep the home and look after the flock. . . . When the minister returned to Savannah, I was so tired I resigned and did not intend ever to go into the work again. . . .

Dr. Welker had invited me to come to his home and teach his children, so I returned to North Carolina. I bought a little fruit farm, the cottage on which was quite near the Welker's. The trees were young—just coming into bearing. . . . I thought, that with fruit and fowls and a garden, I could make a living. I was only three miles from McLeansville so I could see friends there sometimes and hear from them often. Some of the Church members lived near me. So I was very happy in my little home and hoped to spend my remaining days there.

But it was not to be so. Dr. [Joseph E.] Roy, Secretary of the A.M.A., with much pleading made me believe that *duty* called me elsewhere. He said I was not to teach school but to teach the minister and oversee the work of three churches that had colored teachers and an ignorant minister; and do whatever missionary work I found time for.

Thus, in 1885 Esther Douglass loaded her goods on a wagon, left her little farm, and traveled about twenty-five country miles to Oaks, North Carolina, where she spent the next six years of her life. For three years she shared a two-room log cabin with Aunt Nellie, a Black woman, who gave her the better room which had no windows; the only sources of light and heat were the open door and a small fireplace. Before the second winter, however, windows were installed in the room and the church building was far enough along to be used for school, Sunday school, and church meetings.

In 1888 Esther and her blind sister, Emeline, built a house, in which they both lived during the remainder of Esther's years at Oaks. (This house was bought by the American Missionary Association as a parsonage for the Oaks Church.)

One year earlier, in December 1887, she wrote:

Sabbath morning I went to the Baptist Sabbath School. Though they have quite a large church membership, there were but ten scholars in the school. Being asked to talk to them about the lesson, I tried to show them that many of the very common practices among the colored people are not consistent with the spirit of the Sabbath; and that to enforce the truth that we ought never to say, "I can't" in reply to any command of Jesus, for if we make the effort to obey, strength will be given as it was to the withered hand.

At 11 A.M. we had our own meeting in the school house. A sermon was read about the "Precious Blood of Christ." At two P.M. our Sabbath School met in the same place; only 15 were present. A baptism in the river at the same hour drew many away, but most of the regular scholars were there. A young licentiate who was officiating in the Methodist church was in my class. Before we closed he was called out by his church bell. As he passed out he said to our deacon—"We had that lesson in our school this morning, and I did not get the understanding of it. I should like to go and teach it over again." After school we had a Bible reading, and at night a Temperance Bible Reading. Six white young men stood by the window looking in. Finally one said to the others, "She's white, she'll let us come in. I am going right up front where I can hear good." (He spoke so loudly that he was heard, tho' the windows were closed.) They came in, took front seats, and were very attentive. When the invitation was given for any who wished to receive some temperance tracts, they took some.

Was this a typical Sunday—five services, serving as teacher or leader in all of them? The closing paragraph in the same letter states: "An appointment had been given me to be at Melville, but I could get no conveyance. I wish some one would give a covered buggy (I can get horses and drivers in plenty, but nothing to ride in). As an extra gift to the A.M.A., it is much needed."

The buggy came in 1889.

The First Congregational Church in Springfield [Massachusetts] paid my salary so I was obliged to send a report to them every month. When I told of the discomforts of my six-mile journeys, they had built for me a nice, very strong, covered buggy. The carriage and a harness were a present. I bought a horse so my trips were usually very comfortable.

Weekdays as well as Sundays were fully scheduled. In addition to her work in the day school, Esther Douglass was active in all church and community activities at Oaks and made occasional trips (usually by night) to Melville and to Cedar Cliff. In one of her letters, dated July 1889, she wrote: "Monday afternoon the Missionary [Esther herself] had one of her sewing classes in her room and afterwards met about forty of the Sabbath School scholars in the church for practice in preparation for a concert. The object is to raise money to pay a debt on their paster's salary."

In the evening she went to the lyceum conducted by the pastor; she was secretary. This lyceum drew young people from other congregations, and all were allowed to take part in the exercises. Tuesday another sewing class met in the afternoon and at night the church prayer meeting. Wednesday afternoon, women's prayer meeting. Thursday, children's meeting. Friday, once every two weeks, women's missionary meeting and, once a month, the social purity meeting for women and girls. "You will readily see that with preparation for, and attending all these meetings, as well as the distribution of clothing, visiting the sick and other outside work, a Missionary has little time for idleness." Thus, as teacher, home missionary, and friend, Esther W. Douglass for most of her adult life, served underprivileged Blacks in five southern states.

I have told her story at length and have quoted generously from her diary and letters, for she is typical of many white young women and young Congregational ministers who left the comforts and advantages of their northern homes to work among Freedmen—men, women, and children—working through their ignorance, their fears, and their superstitions to true friendship, understanding, and appreciation, teaching them the rudiments of a trained citizenship; lifting their economic and moral standards; leading them to Christ, and preparing them for participation in the work of evangelizing the whole community wherever they had opportunity. These home missionaries were not only commissioned by the American Missionary Association, they were committed Christians. The schools were Christian schools. The Bible was taught as an essential to proper education. The imperatives were not only to educate but also to Christianize all who came to their schools. It was out of the womb of this high dedication to Christ that the Black Congregational churches of the South were born.

The story of Esther Douglass was paralleled at many places across the South—at Dudley, Raleigh, Beaufort, New Bern, and Wilmington, North Carolina; at Beaufort, Charleston, Hilton Head, and St. Helena, South Carolina; at Atlanta, Macon, Ogeechee, and Savannah, Georgia; Athens, Marion, Montgomery, Selma, and Talladega, Alabama; Jackson, Meridian, and Tougaloo, Mississippi; Chattanooga, Memphis, and Nashville, Tennessee; New Orleans, Lockport, Terrebonne, and New Iberia, Louisiana; Brownsville and Corpus Christi, Texas—to name a few select stations. Although many teachers and missionaries experienced the same kinds of hardships, indignities, and self-denials that Esther Douglass experienced, they made the same discoveries of abilities and humanness common to all races and achieved the same results in educating Black people and in Christianizing Black communities.

By 1870 the American Missionary Association had sent out 2,628 teachers and missionaries. Literally, hundreds of schools had been established; at least twenty-six of these were along the coasts of North and South Carolina, Georgia, and Florida. In connection with nearly every day school there was a night school for adults and a Sunday school. It was estimated that at least 131,000 students attended these day schools, and about the same number were enrolled in night schools and in Sunday schools.

For the most part they were true, New England-type Congregational churches, because they were organized initially by New England-type Congregational ministers and missionaries. The first pastors were white; the first Sunday school teachers were missionaries in AMA schools. Many churches were proud to be *the First* Congregational Church in their community or city. Others chose names of northern churches and of famous Congregationalists: Plymouth, Pilgrim, Broadway; Chandler, Beard, Beecher, Gregory, Howard, Hubbard, Woodbury. All started as Congregational churches, indoctrinated with Congregational principles. Their covenants and constitutions (if any) were patterned after northern churches. They adhered to the Congregational Manual as to organization, structure, sacraments, and ordinances of the church.

Early Congregational missionaries made every attempt to

evangelize; they made no attempt to proselytize. At evangelistic services converts were asked to choose the church they would attend, and many chose Baptist or Methodist churches. Intelligence in worship, in the understanding of the Bible, and in the application of truth in matters of personal conduct and social intercourse was emphasized. These churches became "lighthouses" in their respective communities, and although often accused of being quiet, unemotional, and highbrow, they furnished far more than their share of community leadership in education, in moral uplift, and in economic and social progress, as well as in the ministries of the church.

Perhaps the American Missionary Association's most significant act for Black churches was the establishment of theological seminaries or departments of religious training at the major centers of learning. While Bible and religion were taught in all AMA schools of this early period, seminaries or religious departments were established at Fisk University, Talladega College, Tougaloo College, Straight College, and at schools in Memphis, Tennessee and in Atlanta, Georgia. For half a century the majority of Black Congregational ministers were trained in one of these schools. The association schools were feeders for these seminaries and religious centers. Ministerial students came from all over the South and from many denominational backgrounds. Most of them came with little or no education, little or no money, but none was turned away. They were given quite limited financial assistance; they brought corn, sweet potatoes, and other farm products; they worked on college farms and campuses and were determined to make their way, to stay in school, and to get an education. Many of these ministerial students were encouraged by their religious teachers to establish mission Sunday schools and churches and were given any needed assistance and supervision in these projects. At first, even in the colleges, entrance requirements were a genuine desire for an education and a willingness to work.

In the early years AMA colleges were colleges in name only. Training began in the primary grades and, in time, advanced to a full four-year college course. Sources of students, other than AMA schools in the South, were almost nil. The same was true of ministerial students. They started at whatever educational level, if any, they had attained and climbed the ladder of religious or theological training. If and when they reached the top of the ladder, they were awarded college and seminary degrees; but there were lower rungs, various levels from which they could step off; for instance, after creditable completion of an English Bible course. This is the way that nearly all Black Congregational ministers were trained, and it was they or their northern white predecessors who organized and served the Black churches.

One of the first seminaries to open and the last to close was at Talladega College, Talladega, Alabama. It was there, in 1868, that the First Congregational Church was organized and that training for preachers was advertised. This brought together eighteen students for the ministry who were but three years out of slavery. By 1872 ten churches could be counted as the direct outgrowth of the First Church of Talladega. A distinct department of theology was opened in 1873. According to George W. Andrews, reporting in the *Talladegan* in 1892, nearly two hundred ministers had received their training in this theological department, and many had served several denominations.

Dr. Andrews was the moving spirit in the development of the theological department at Talladega and in the organization of Black Congregational churches in Alabama. He is credited with having established eight churches, the Alabama Congregational Conference, and the Alabama Sunday School Convention. From 1870 to 1908, except for one year (1872), he was missionary in Alabama for the American Missionary Association. For thirty-four of these years he was dean and professor of theology at Talladega College; for ten years (1894–1904) he also served as president of the college. When he retired, in 1908, he was made professor emeritus. No other person did more to train Black ministers in the South and to establish Congregationalism among Black people than Dr. Andrews. Within ten years after he retired, graduates of the theological department of Talladega College, under the leadership of the Rev. William H. Holloway, an alumnus, started campaigning for a building to be erected on the campus of Talladega College to be "known forever as 'Andrews Theological Hall.'"

What was accomplished at Talladega College was being duplicated in lesser degree, at Fisk, Tougaloo, and Straight. Students who were being trained for the Christian ministry gained field experience by serving communities and by organizing churches within workable radii of these institutions. Thus, many Congregational churches were organized in Tennessee, Mississippi, Louisiana, and Alabama. The most productive of these seminaries was at Talladega. Twenty years after it was begun, the department of Bible and theological study reported seventy-five graduates, most of whom were serving or had served as pastors of "important churches from Savannah to San Francisco." The course of study was rearranged and enlarged from time to time, so that by 1892 those who completed college and full seminary requirements received the bachelor of divinity degree. In 1872, when theological training began at Talladega, there was not a single Black Congregational minister in Alabama, and there were only three Black Congregational churches in the state. By 1892 there were thirty-three Black Congregational churches in Alabama, being served by ministers who had completed courses in Bible and theological study at Talladega. Seven of these ministers had fulfilled the requirements for the bachelor of divinity degree.

Many graduates of American Missionary Association schools in the South were encouraged by their teachers to go to Talladega College or elsewhere for further training. Later, some returned to their native communities to become pastors of Black Congregational churches.

Reporting in *The Pilgrim* (October 1893) J.E. Roy, secretary of the American Missionary Association, stated that

the Sunday Schools of the AMA number 18,080 scholars. Every church and every day school has its Sunday School and many of them have their mission Sunday schools in regions round about. In this way the larger institutions such as Tougaloo and Talladega are running several Sunday schools, and out of these have come, and still are coming, church organizations, themselves in turn to start other Sunday schools that in time will come on to the maturity of church life.

In an 1895 issue of the same publication an article written by Dr.

Roy titled "The Last Decade of the AMA Work in the South (1885–1895)" stated that

> in this period our churches among the colored people have come on in numbers from 57 to 143; in members from 6,164 to 10,000. The Sunday school scholars in these churches have advanced from 13,150 to 17,015. Money contributed for church uses has increased from $10,660 to $29,545; benevolent contributions from $1,020 to $4,332. . . . We have just heard of the earnest intent and endeavor of these churches to come forward to self-support, as have the Plymouth of Charleston, and the churches of Savannah, Memphis, Atlanta, Chattanooga and others.

Within a score of years after the Civil War, Black Congregational churches had been organized in every southern state. The number of these churches continued to increase through the first decade of the twentieth century.

Chapter 4

Beginnings and Early Development of the Black Christian Church

Although records for the beginning years are almost nonexistent, 1865 seems to be the year that Negro Christian churches first were established. One must turn to the *Annual* of the American Christian Convention, *The Herald*, Milo True Morrill's *History of the Christian Denomination in America, 1794-1911, The Christian Sun,* and other white publications. Even in these sources, information is limited, and much research is required to find the answers. According to Morrill, the first Christian church with an all-Black membership was Providence Church, of Norfolk (Chesapeake), Virginia. This church was dedicated on June 4, 1854; the number of charter members is unknown. Membership was made up of free men and slaves who had worshiped in the balconies of white Christian churches in Virginia. The first pastor of this church was white, and sympathetic whites gave instruction and guidance in organizing the church and in developing Black leadership. This church is still very much in existence, but no statistics or early records can be found.

The Civil War ended in the spring of 1865. As early as fall of the same year Black Christian churches were being formed at points in North Carolina and in Virginia. While only two Negro Christian churches date their beginning in 1865—Broad Creek, of Oriental, North Carolina, and Christian Home, of Apex, North Carolina—it is reasonable to assume that many other churches started in 1865 and in 1866.

According to the *Christian Annual*, "The North Carolina Colored Christian Conference [originally named the Western North Carolina Conference] was organized in the city of Raleigh, in 1866. . . . The Rev. Wm. M. Hayes was the first president." Twelve ministers and twenty churches were represented in this meeting, and the conference included all Black Christian ministers and churches of North Carolina and of Virginia. The Rev. W.B. Wellons, the Rev. J.W. Wellons, and the Rev. H.B.

Hayes, white ministers of the General Christian Convention, ably assisted the "colored brethren" in organizing churches of their own and in the organization of the colored conference, in keeping with the cardinal principles of the Christian platform. These three men gave direction in the ordination of the first Black ministers, and for a decade or more they attended the sessions of the colored conferences as fraternal messengers of the white Christian convention and shared generously in the discussions and transactions of the conferences. Along with other white Christian ministers, they organized several Negro churches and served as their first pastors.

The decade of 1865–75 was one of pioneering and expansion. Brush arbors, log cabins, and abandoned animal shelters were the first housing for many churches. It is remarkable that from these lowly beginnings consecrated Black leaders, with limited training and very limited resources, could preach the gospel, build church buildings of a sort, organize new churches, and add members to those that already existed. The 1873 session of the conference, held at Christian Chapel in Wake County, North Carolina, listed twenty-seven ministers. The number of churches was not given. The Rev. Brutus Young and the Rev. S.L. Long were elected president and secretary, respectively. The Rev. A. Apple, the Rev. J.W. Wellons, and the Rev. W.G. Clements were fraternal messengers from the white convention.

A new conference had been formed in eastern North Carolina. At this 1873 session "it was decided that the body in session should hereafter be called the Western North Carolina Conference, and the new Conference be called the Eastern North Carolina Conference. . . . The dividing line between the two Conferences, is the Wilmington and Weldon Railroad." The next session of the Eastern North Carolina Conference was to be held at Spring Green Church, Washington County, on the Thursday before the fourth Sunday in September 1874; of the Western North Carolina Conference at White's Grove, Warren County, on the Wednesday before the second Sunday in November 1874.

Also at the 1873 session "the Conference decided to assess the membership of the Churches for a sufficient amount to put a High School at Franklinton in operation."

50

On Thursday, December 11, 1873 the ministers and delegates from the Black Christian churches met at Mount Ararat, Nansemond County, Virginia, for the "purpose of organizing a Conference." Fraternal messengers who gave assistance were the Rev. W.B. Wellons, the Rev. J.N. Manning, and the Rev. E.W. Beale. The Rev. Justin Copeland was the first president. Elisha A. Copeland was chosen secretary. Originally, this conference was composed of six churches, two ordained ministers, and six licentiates. Church membership was not given. The next session of the Eastern Virginia Conference was held at Zion Church, also in Nansemond County, near Holland, on the Friday before the fourth Sunday in October 1874.

Thus, within ten years three Black Christian conferences had been formed in North Carolina and in Virginia—the Western North Carolina Colored Christian Conference, the Eastern North Carolina Colored Christian Conference, and the Eastern Virginia Colored Christian Conference. In 1874 the Western North Carolina Conference had twenty-three ministers and about thirty-five churches; the Eastern North Carolina, eleven ministers and nine churches; and Eastern Virginia, seven ministers and seven churches. According to these figures, at the end of the first decade there were forty-one ministers and fifty-one churches in North Carolina and in Virginia. Churches had developed around such centers as Raleigh, Burlington, Henderson, and New Bern, North Carolina; and Norfolk and Holland, Virginia. The *Christian Annual* makes frequent reference to the missionary zeal of white Christian ministers, under appointment from their conference, who organized churches "among colored people," gave instruction to Black leaders, and sometimes presided over church and conference meetings. The 1871 edition of the *Christian Annual* states that the "Rev. W.B. Wellons and the Rev. R.H. Holland preside over and counsel with the colored ministers and churches, under appointment from the Conference. . . . The Rev. M.B. Barrett preaches for a congregation of colored people in Southampton County [Virginia] and the Rev. S.S. Barrett will probably organize several colored churches in the vicinity of Norfolk soon." Similar action on the part of white ministers in North Carolina is cited in the *Christian Annual*.

The historic background of the multiple origin, the development and growth of the Christian denomination, and its cardinal principles and polity were carried over into the colored Christian church and were duly accepted and adhered to as was the *Manual* of the Christian denomination. Vestiges of the denominations from which the Christians moved for doctrinal reasons also carried over into the Black churches.

Conferences were largely controlled by their officers or an Elders' Council. "Christ was Head," but at times not the only head of the local church. This authority might be exercised by the pastor, the head deacon, or a board of officers.

During these first ten years certain Blacks stand out as organizers, as pastors, and as conference leaders. The Rev. William M. Hayes, one of the first Blacks to be ordained, was the first president of the Western North Carolina Conference and was one of the leading pastors of his day. Also helping to organize new churches and serving as pastors in that conference were the Rev. R.I. Johnson, the Rev. Jackson Jeffreys, and the Rev. J.S. Harris, all of Raleigh. The Rev. Brutus Young, Ridgeway, North Carolina, succeeded Hayes as president of the conference. He and the Rev. Thomas Bullock organized and served churches along the state line, between North Carolina and Virginia.

The first president of the Eastern Virginia Conference was the Rev. Justin Copeland. He also had charge of three young churches—Mount Ararat, Zion, and Antioch. The Rev. Louis Darden, organizer of the Corinth Church (still one of the leading rural churches of Virginia), was the first pastor and the builder of that church's first building, a log structure with a thatch roof. He had already begun the erection of a slightly more adequate frame building when he died. The building was completed by his successor, Justin Copeland. Other outstanding ministers of this early period were the Rev. Henry Hamlin, the Rev. Jacob Skeeter, and the Rev. Jesse Jones. Talitha Briggs was licensed for the ministry and served among the churches in the Suffolk area. She was probably the first Black woman to be licensed by any Negro conference.

The Rev. Joseph H. Mann Sr. was the first president of the Eastern North Carolina Conference. He organized the Broad Creek Church, in Pamlico County, the oldest church in the conference. Small's Chapel was named for its founder and builder of its first house of worship, the Rev. A. Small, who was also vice-president and treasurer of the conference. The Rev. J.H. Milteer and the Rev. F.L. Taylor were among the old-timers who helped to organize churches and to build their first buildings. The leading church, one of the oldest, was Watson's Chapel, of New Bern. Later, its name was changed to West Street Church. This church was organized by the Rev. A. Watson. These five men played a prominent role in the establishment of the Eastern North Carolina Conference. At one time or another, each one either shared in the organization and building or served as pastor of every church in the conference that was organized during the nineteenth century.

In an address recorded in full in the minutes of the 25th Session of the Afro-Christian Convention, held at Wesley Grove Christian Church, Newport News, Virginia on June 20-28, 1916, Mann made the following statements:

I think we organized two conferences . . . and not one of the members besides myself is living. . . . My first knowledge of the Christian Church was about sixty years ago. It was then I connected with the Christian Church. I have baptized a thousand souls to the Christian Faith. I have built 19 churches and done what I could.

I have had to go 25 to 30 miles to a church through wind and snow, and had to swim the creek with my clothes on my head, but I went just the same. I had been preaching three years and in that three years I did not get but three dollars. They told me that licensed preachers did not need any pay.

Now you see how we got along, but we banded ourselves together and we formed a Conference, and this is our first minute. [He held up a copy of the minutes.]

Well it does me good to look at you now! As I said before, I have done what I could. I baptized over a thousand souls, built 19 churches, and laid the foundation for Franklinton Christian College.

This is typical of the glorious spirit and the personal sacrifices of the founders of Black Christian churches and conferences. Those named above were leaders of distinction in their fields of work. Many who remain unnamed followed their leadership and went out to organize and to build churches of "the Christian Faith." Some churches were built of logs; most were shabby little one-room buildings. But in the most trying times and under the most difficult circumstances, with very limited resources, they "did what they could." Together they made the period from 1865 to 1875 and the quarter century that followed the golden period in the history of Black Christian churches.

By 1900 several significant events had taken place. Many new churches had been established, the number of ministers had increased, and more young men were asking for licensure. Additional church buildings of better quality were being erected. Most of the churches had set up Sunday schools for Bible study and for the training of children and youth. The women and the Sunday schools had been organized into conventions. New conferences had been formed, and the Afro-Christian Convention, composed of all conferences of the Black Christian churches, was a reality. In spite of humble and uncertain beginnings, the school at Franklinton, North Carolina became Franklinton Christian College.

The old conferences grew rapidly. The Western North Carolina Conference reclaimed its original name—the North Carolina Colored Christian Conference. It boasted a total of fifty-eight churches, thirty-three of which were rural or country churches. Twenty-three of these churches had full-time (every Sunday) preaching services. Most other churches had preaching services only once each month, usually both morning and night services. Fifty-three of the churches reported property ranging in value from $50 to $2,200. The total membership of the churches was 3,952. Fifty-three Sunday schools and three Christian Endeavor societies had been formed. There were thirty-seven ordained ministers and eighteen licentiates in the conference. Outstanding churches, on the basis of memberships that exceeded one hundred, were Antioch, near Townsville, North Carolina; Burchett's Chapel, near Manson, North Carolina; Cary Christian, Cary, North Carolina; Children's Chapel, Graham, North Carolina; Franklinton Christian, Franklinton, North Carolina; Jerusalem, near Palmer Springs, Virginia; Oak Level, near Manson, North Carolina; Pleasant Union, near Raleigh, North Carolina; Poplar Springs, also near Raleigh; and White's Grove, near Norlina, North Carolina. Most of these were rural churches, and some are still among the leading Black churches of North Carolina. Again, if judged by the size of membership, with rare exception, the Black Christian churches that are continuing to do notable work and to improve the quality and quantity of worship and services in their communities were organized in the nineteenth century. Most of the organizers of these churches were born slaves and had limited training. Many of them had experienced balcony worship in white Christian churches, from which they received their name and polity, their missionary zeal for church extension and the "saving of souls," and patterns of organizational structures. They were not always certain of their denominational identity.

Infant baptism was rarely practiced; adult baptism was only by emersion. Because of a lack of pools the early churches used creeks, rivers, or ponds for this purpose.

Pastoral "appointments" were read out at each annual conference. Elders' councils, presbyteries, and stewards were frequently used designations. Apparent in all Black Christian churches and conferences were emotional intensities and styles of preaching, praying, and singing that were inherently African.

By the end of the nineteenth century the Eastern North Carolina Conference had become the Eastern Atlantic Christian Conference. The conference continued under this name until the organization of the Southern Conference of the United Church of Christ in 1965. Statistics published in 1900 in the *Herald of Gospel Liberty* indicated twelve churches with a combined membership of 865 and property value totaling $8,300 (five of these churches reported no property). There were nine ordained ministers, eight licentiates, two Christian Endeavor societies, and ten Sunday schools. Two of these churches had preaching services twice each month; the other ten only once per month.

In 1900 the *Herald of Gospel Liberty* report for the Eastern Virginia Conference was made by the conference secretary, W.T. Howell. Of the twenty-six churches listed, twenty-two were classified as country churches, including the four leading churches—Corinth Chapel, Chapel Grove, Zion, and Laurel

Hill—which had a combined membership of over 900. The total membership of the conference was 2,218. Twenty-four churches owned property ranging in value from $100 to $6,000; total property value reported was $24,700. There were twenty-three Sunday schools, twenty-one ordained ministers, and seventeen licentiates, one of whom was a woman. By this time Justin Copeland had retired, and many young people were on the scene, working faithfully to establish Black Christian churches and to increase church membership.

At the turn of the century the Rev. Smith Allen Howell was pastor of Corinth Chapel, of Franklin, and Wesley Grove, of Newport News. Corinth Chapel then had the largest membership—262—of any of the Black churches in Virginia. During his pastorate, which lasted over fifty years, Howell remodeled and beautified the building he found there; and when this became too small for his growing congregation, a beautiful, spacious, well-arranged church was built to replace it. Older members of the church describe this building as "the finest wood structure" anywhere in the area, and they still speak of Howell as their most beloved pastor.

Howell became pastor of Wesley Grove Christian Church in January 1897 and served until 1929. Within four years, because of rapid membership growth, the church was "forced to buy more lots and build a much more spacious building to accommodate members and friends. This new building was 50 by 90 feet, with gallery all around and a seating capacity of 1000 persons. . . . Under the leadership of Rev. Howell the church grew and prospered and attained its largest membership of more than 1000."

The Rev. F.R. Jordan was also prominent among the Virginia ministers. He was the conference president and the pastor of Zion and Laurel Hill, of Holland; Mount Ararat, of Suffolk; and Chapel Grove, of Windsor—four of the leading rural churches of Virginia, which claimed nearly one third of the state's membership. Other well-known Virginia pastors of this era were Isaiah Dillard, at Bethany, Mercy Seat, and Windsor Grove; J.J. Faulk, at Providence and St. Luke; W.S. Matthews, at Holly Springs and New Hope; J.M. Parsons, at Antioch, Homeville, and Pleasant Grove; and J.S. Sumler, at Providence and St.

Luke. Together these seven men served eighteen of the twenty-six Virginia churches and 1,991 of the 2,218 members. The other eight churches were new churches and for the most part were served by licentiates, who were required to organize a church as a prerequisite to ordination. Several churches, such as Holly Springs, Lone Starr, Mercy Seat, Parson Hill, St. Martha's Chapel, and St. Stevens, no longer appear in the Virginia records, but their influence remained and Black Christian churches continued to grow in southeast tidewater Virginia.

By 1896 there were five conferences. The Eastern North Carolina Conference had become the Eastern Atlantic Christian Conference; the Western North Carolina Conference had returned to its original name—the North Carolina Colored Christian Conference. The Eastern Virginia Conference continued under the same name.

The Cape Fear Conference is mentioned in the reports of the 1874 meeting of the Western North Carolina Conference, but nowhere can any records of this conference be found. It is probable that this was a conference of Black Christian Disciple churches located along the coastal area of North Carolina, from Wilmington to Washington. At both the 1873 and 1874 sessions of the Western North Carolina Conference "Fraternal Messengers were received from a Conference in the Eastern part of the State." This conference included both Christian and Christian Disciple churches. There were irreconcilable doctrinal differences and disagreement on the "Christian Platform," and the two groups drifted apart. As late as 1916 the statistical table for the Eastern Atlantic Conference, published in the *Proceedings and Journal* (minutes of the 1916 session held at Wesley Grove, Newport News, Virginia) of the Afro-Christian Convention, lists twenty-six churches. Ten of these churches made no report and were not represented in the convention by pastors or delegates. They also had no identification or association in the Eastern Atlantic Christian Conference. The Cape Fear Conference was never a conference of the Afro-Christian Churches.

The Georgia-Alabama Colored Christian Conference was organized in 1887. Although very little is known of this conference, it is listed among the annual conferences in the 1916 minutes of the Afro-Christian Convention. The Rev. Oscar F.

Gunn, the Rev. P.S. Phillips, and E. Jenkins were listed respectively as president, vice-president, and secretary, but there was no report from the conference. Several Black churches were established along the central state line of western Georgia and of eastern Alabama, where there were many white Christian churches. One Black Christian church is still in existence: the Sweet Home Christian Church, of Roanoke, Alabama. No trace of any other church of the Georgia-Alabama Colored Christian Conference was ever found.

The Lincoln Conference, also listed in the 1916 Afro-Christian Convention minutes, was organized in 1910. It included a group of Christian churches, formerly members of the North Carolina Colored Christian Conference, which, for reasons of travel and entertainment and by mutual agreement with the parent conference, formed their own conference. Nearly all Lincoln Conference churches were within a radius of thirty miles of Burlington, North Carolina.

The Pennsylvania, New Jersey, and New York Christian Conference was organized in 1912. In 1916, in the Afro-Christian Convention minutes, this conference listed sixteen ministers (unclassified) and five churches—four in New York and one in New Jersey. The 1936 *Year Book* of the Congregational Christian Churches registers a total of ten churches—six in New York and four in New Jersey. In neither instance is a church in Pennsylvania listed. Total membership reported in 1936 was 372.

Also, in the same minutes of the Afro-Christian Convention there is mention of a British Guiana, South America Conference and a "Ministerial Directory of the British Guiana, S.A., and the Trinidad, B.W.I. Conferences." Statistics showed four mission churches in British Guiana, one mission church in Trinidad, British West Indies, and a mission school with an enrollment of 150. The four churches in South America were all in Demerara County, British Guiana, and the conference was referred to as the Demerara Conference of South America. The "whole number of members as recently reported for the South American work (was) 945." But this total was the aggregate of members of the churches, the women's home mission groups, the schools, and the Christian Endeavor societies. Certain missionaries and their respective fields were indicated: the Rev. J.A. Johnson,

Barbados, British West Indies; the Rev. E.J. Bernard, Trinidad, British West Indies; and the Rev. W. Gill, Jamaica, British West Indies.

According to Morrill, the Rev. William Hazel, a minister of the North Carolina Colored Christian Conference, was doing great work in Tennessee, and in 1875 he was deputized to organize a colored Christian conference there. No other mention of work in that state has been found.

The latest conference to be formed was the Southern District Conference. Like the Lincoln Conference, it was a division of the North Carolina Colored Christian Conference. It was necessary to make these divisions for the purpose of housing and entertaining those who attended the conference gatherings. Private homes had to be used for housing; meals were served in the homes or on the grounds of the entertaining church during the time the conference was in session, usually four to six days. Generally, major expenses of this entertainment were borne by the host church.

Mainly for the same reasons, the Eastern Virginia Conference divided into the Eastern Virginia and the Western Virginia conferences, the Atlantic Coastline Railroad serving as a dividing line between east and west. While the territory of the two conferences did not overlap, most Virginia ministers were members of both conferences; some also served churches in both conferences. Indeed, a few Virginia ministers, by paying the required dues, were enrolled as members of one or more of the North Carolina conferences and frequently served churches in that area also. The same was true of some North Carolina ministers in relation to Virginia conferences and churches.

In North Carolina the only exclusive conference area was that of the Eastern Atlantic Conference. The geographical areas of the other three conferences overlapped. Title to the property of a number of churches was held by the North Carolina Colored Christian Conference (the parent conference), and as new conferences were formed, these titles were transferred to the new conferences or to the churches themselves. There was excellent cooperation and regular exchange of fraternal messengers between conferences. Again, many ministers were members of two or more conferences, and a few held office in at least two of the conferences. Despite the divisions that created the Lincoln and the Southern District conferences, the North Carolina Conference continued to be the largest and most influential Black Christian conference.

The Afro-Christian Convention was organized at Watson's Tabernacle in New Bern, North Carolina. The organization was the general convention of all Afro-Christian conferences, churches, and ministers of the "United States of America, Canada, South America and the West Indies." There was great ambition but little reality in this title. The date of organization for the convention is uncertain. According to its minutes, the "Semi-Centennial" Biennial Session of the convention was held at Wesley Grove Christian Church, Newport News, Virginia, June 20-28, 1916. It is hardly possible that the convention was organized in 1866, when there was only one conference and very few churches. The most probable date is 1892, as given in Morrill's *History of the Christian Denomination,* although the *American Christian Annual* states that the Afro-Christian Convention was organized in May 1902.

No minutes or records of the convention dated earlier than 1916 have been found. A vivid description of the later years of the Afro-Christian Convention (1914-50) is given in a letter written by the Rev. Joseph D. Farrar, Newport News, Virginia, under date of March 26, 1966.

As far as my memory will go . . . my first visit to the Afro-Christian Convention was made in 1914 in Durham, North Carolina at the White Rock Christian Church. At that time, the Rev. J.A. Holloway was presiding.

Then the tide was very low, so low that we had to reorganize. Then we made Dr. S.A. Howell President, and there, you might say, we began a new Afro Convention. Howell then took over and blew the little flame that was left until it became a pretty good fire. It operated its own printing press, resurrected Franklinton School on Highway #1.

Howell served some 20 years or more, during which time the Afro Convention was in splendor. Succeeding him was the Rev. C.A. Harris who served a few years; and succeeding him was the Rev. I.D.C. Goodson. During his time the Afro Convention again almost lost its head way.

The light was very dim.

Then I, your humble servant, J.D. Farrar, was elected President. I served some 12 years, and gave up at Franklinton. And the Rev. Mr. Hargett was elected in my stead. And I believe in the next year we organized the Convention of the South.

The 1916 minutes show that the convention had reached a maturity that was highly impressive. The Rev. Smith A. Howell, D.D., of Newport News, Virginia, was president of the convention. The Rev. F.L. Taylor and the Rev. Charles A. Harris were vice-president and recording secretary; they were also presidents of the Eastern Atlantic and Eastern Virginia conferences respectively. The Rev. J.E. Samuels was general superintendent of the session. The minutes were published by The Afro-Christian Publishing Association, Franklinton, North Carolina.

In his biennial address at the 1916 session of the convention, President Howell stated that

this Convention is composed of seven annual Conferences including our foreign fields, with an aggregate membership of twenty-five thousand and with their various auxiliaries have raised for all purposes during the biennium nearly fifty thousand dollars. There are 153 churches with an equal number of Sunday Schools and Christian Endeavor Societies and about 185 ordained Elders and Licentiates.

The Sunday School Conventions control the constituency of about 12 thousand scholars and about one thousand officers and teachers. . . . The Woman's National Home and Foreign Missionary Convention takes in all of the various State Conventions and Unions and is destined to be an organization of wide influence and a powerful factor in the development of the women of our church.

Chapter 5

Franklinton Christian College

The most significant achievement of the Christian denomination that benefited Black Christians was the development of a school at Franklinton, North Carolina, which, in time, became Franklinton Christian College. As early as 1871 a school for "colored people" was opened in the Black Christian church of Franklinton by a white Christian minister from Illinois. Black children and some women were enrolled in the same classes in the day school. There were night classes for working mothers and Black men. The church building was small and woefully overcrowded both day and night, so eager were children and adults to learn to read and write.

According to the minutes, the 1871 annual session of the North Carolina Colored Christian Conference was held at Burchett's Chapel, Manson, North Carolina, November 9–11. Seven elders and lay delegates from ten churches were present. At this session of the conference "the propriety of establishing a High School at Franklinton was discussed at length, and Norfleet White, S.L. Long and Wm. M. Hayes [were] appointed a committee to purchase a lot and take steps at once, for the establishment of such a school. Two hundred and fifty-four dollars was raised at once for the school."

At the 1873 session of the conference, held "at Christian Chapel in Wake County, the Conference decided to assess the membership of the churches for a sufficient amount to put a High School at Franklinton in Operation." The concern for education and for a school at Franklinton persisted in this and other Black conferences in North Carolina and in Virginia. Church members were assessed (usually ten cents per member) and offerings were received at each conference session. But the postwar South was poor, especially the ex-slave, Black South, so that money for buying a site, erecting a school building, and paying teachers' salaries was extremely difficult to provide.

The first site for the school was purchased for $300. It was situated on the south side of the town, between Main Street and the railroad, but for lack of buildings the school continued to operate in the church. "At a conference held at New Bern, North Carolina, October 31, 1877 . . . it was recommended that each member of the Church be assessed 10¢ a year for the establishment of a high school at Franklinton, North Carolina, and in the fall of the year, 1878, the school was opened by Prof. Henry E. Long in the old Franklinton Christian Church."

In 1880 two important things happened. The Rev. George W. Dunn, a former slave, began writing letters to the editor of the *Herald of Gospel Liberty* describing the poverty and illiteracy of his people and appealing for financial and material aid. His letters were published in the *Herald*. Help from northern Christians was immediate, and soon the first building was erected. In the fall of 1880 the school moved to its new location. The title to the school property was placed in the hands of the American Christian Convention, and a board of directors (or board of control) was appointed to manage the affairs of the institution.

Also in the fall of 1880 the Rev. George Young, a young white minister of the Eastern Christian Conference of New York, was sent to Franklinton by the mission board of the American Christian Convention and became principal of the school. Professor Long became his assistant.

The *Herald of Gospel Liberty* continued to carry detailed reports of the Franklinton School and appeals for the support of the school. Many northern churches, women's organizations, and Sunday schools, as well as individuals, pledged support, and many gave both cash and material gifts. Lists of these gifts were published frequently in the *Herald*. Perhaps the best description of the school and its facilities, its teachers, and the effectiveness of its work can be found in letters that appeared in the *Herald of Gospel Liberty*.

From a letter written on April 2, 1883 by the Rev. John G. Wilson, Philadelphia:

Having furnished means for the building of the Gaylord Boarding Hall in connection with the Franklinton School, and the same being nearly finished, Mrs. Wilson proposed that we should visit the place, and see how the institution was progressing. We left home, January 25, 1883, stopping in Baltimore a few days with our kind and dear friends, Rev. A. Webster, D.D., and family. . . . Monday, 29th, we went to Washington. . . . We went to the Capitol and saw both houses of Congress in disorderly session. Visited the Louise Home, founded by the great banker Corcoran. Also attended the President's levee. We thought he seemed annoyed by the hand-shaking and considered it a decided bore. . . .

Thursday, February 1st, we reached Franklinton, and were met at the station by Rev. George Young, Principal of the School, and Rev. J.W. Wellons, who conducted us to the principal's cottage where we were cordially entertained during our stay. After supper we attended a religious service in the school building, when one of the Theological class preached, evidently under considerable embarrassment. The matter and manner was the subject of criticism by his fellow-students in the class the next day, softened by the apologetic remarks of the principal, at whose request we gave them an address on ministerial work, etc. On Friday, February 2, we attended the exercises of the school throughout the day, and at suitable times spoke words of encouragement and exhortation to all.

The school buildings occupy the most eligible site in the village. . . . The ground is sufficiently elevated to command a prospect of the entire village, and large enough for the building of a first class college and campus which it may some day become. At all events it bids fair to attain the rank of the Literary and Theological Institute of the North Carolina and Virginia African Conferences of the Christian Denomination, and they may in time be able to sustain it, but at present the means for building purposes, and to pay the principal and his assistants must mainly come from the North, and should be given without stint.

The school building and lot on which it stands were paid for by subscriptions to the Franklinton School Fund. They cost about $2,500, and are held in trust by the American Christian Convention for use of the school. The building is a frame structure, 50 by 30 feet, two stories and dormitory on third floor, with cupola and bell. It has quite an imposing appearance. On the first floor is Brush Hall, which, besides its school purposes, is used as a chapel for religious services. The passage and stairway occupy the remainder of this floor. The second story, besides the passage, has two halls and a class room and library room. But the dormitory is not finished, and the whole interior needs a coat of paint, all of which will require an outlay of $225.

The principal's cottage is south of the school building on an adjoining lot purchased by the colored people and held by trustees appointed by their Conferences. The money to build the cottage was given by them. It is a one-story building, without cellar, garret, or closet, and containing sitting room, two bed rooms, and a kitchen. . . . In it the principal and his assistants reside during the school term. . . .

The Gaylord Boarding Hall is northeast of the school building, on an adjoining lot north of the school lot. The building is 50 by 30 feet, two story and finished garret. It is, or will be, finished and furnished, and as soon as proper arrangements are made, will be conveyed to a Board of Trustees appointed by the Christian Conferences, duly incorporated.

The northwest corner of this lot will make a suitable site for a church, and it is contemplated by the colored people to erect one there.

The condition of the school itself is excellent, and the advancement of the pupils is rapid, so that it has a good reputation. Another season the number of pupils will be considerably increased by the removal from Franklinton of the state normal school for colored teachers; and as the rooms are crowded now, they will be too much crowded. This will make an addition to the building a necessity. . . .

The support of the principal and his assistants is an item of great importance. The amount contributed by the friends North for the present term is, or is expected to be, eight hundred dollars, from all other sources less than two hundred dollars, and with this amount, less than a thousand dollars in all, the principal has to bear the expenses of the school, pay the four assistant teachers, defray all traveling expenses and his own salary. . . .

Some of the Christian denomination, but very few in comparison, have extended the helping hand to these poor and grateful people, and by what has been done have awakened expectations and trust which it would be sad to disappoint. Let all take hold and contribute according to their ability to make this school what it ought to be, that God may be glorified in your liberality and professed subjection to the gospel of Christ.

In a July 1883 issue of the *Herald of Gospel Liberty,* the Rev. W.G. Clements, pastor of a white Christian church in Wake County, wrote:

For some of the Brethren and sisters of the North who have given material aid to the colored Christians of North Carolina, I thought it might be of interest to these donors to know that the Lord was blessing their efforts to do good. Having been raised up among the colored people, and having watched their progress since the Civil War, I think I can speak advisedly as regards their improvements, and I do not hesitate to say, when we take into consideration the means at their command, they have made fair improvements. There is much ignorance among them yet, but where they have had an opportunity of going to school they have generally learned very well.

Bro. Young at Franklinton School is doing a great work. No one but Bro. Young knows the sacrifices he is making for the colored Christians. . . . Those who have given their money to this institution of learning have done a great work.

The colored Christians have considerable numbers in my county, and I see and know many of them. I preach for them whenever I can in this and other counties. A few Sundays ago I was in the town of Graham, N.C., and preached to the white brethren during the day. At night I went out with Bro. D.A. Long to the colored church, and preached for him to the colored brethren. It was the first time I ever preached in a horse stable, for they have to worship in an old brick stable. I thought, if my blessed Savior could condescend to be born in a stable, I ought to be willing to preach his gospel in a stable when it became necessary. Bro. Long is doing a fine work among these brethren, and soon he will have a good house for them to worship in, and they will not be forced to worship in the horse stable.

In August 1883 the Rev. D.L. Putnam wrote of the Franklinton School:

This school is no longer an experiment. A fine location, suitable buildings, and three years of school, in which there has been with each successive year an increasing interest and a permanent growth in numbers, have placed Franklinton permanently among the institutions that be. The work done has been excellent, equal to that of any institution of its character and advantages. The proficiency made in the studies in the academic and Theological departments has been highly commended. The school and teachers at first were looked upon with suspicion and disfavor by a few, but now have "honor in their own country" and have grown in favor wherever known. [The Franklinton School] is a great power for good. . . . It should be esteemed a privilege to hold up the arms of an institution which carries not only educational advantages, but the gospel to the poor. We should not, indeed, we cannot afford to let this branch wither and lose its efficiency for good for the want of proper care and nourishment.

The school was incorporated in 1883 under the name of Franklinton Literary and Theological Christian Institute. As noted earlier, a cottage that housed the principal and his assistants was built on a lot bought by the Black conferences. The Gaylord Boarding Hall was financed by Emily Wilson, of Philadelphia, and was named in honor of her father, Henderson Gaylord.

The quality of work done in the school and the hardships associated with it were vividly described by many who visited the school. But no descriptions are more informing than excerpts from a letter written by Principal George Young in 1883, after three years of work at Franklinton.

We found all the pupils in the rough and crude condition of a race lately emancipated from a debasing slavery, yet earnestly seeking an education. We admit all ages and conditions, requiring no more than good moral character, application to study, and obedience to our rules, as requisites to a stay at the school. In ages, the pupils range from five to forty-five years—the father and the mother and the children all attending, and in some instances the children far ahead of the parents. We turn none away because of his or her poverty. I think I can safely say that in all the families of the 225 pupils that have been under my instructions during the past three years, there is not $40,000 worth of property. They are accumulating every year, but under such adverse circumstances it is very slow.

A brief statement may not be out of place right here. During the past year, not more than $125 was received from the pupils as tuition. This sum, with the $700 given by Bro. Brush [Rev. J.E. Brush, financial agent for the school], is all that I, as principal of the school, received. With this we have paid the current expenses of the school, and paid my assistant teachers. It required about $200 for transportation of teachers to and from Franklinton. The current expenses were about $50. This leaves a very small amount for teachers' salaries.

In the school you will find pupils in their A, B, C's, etc., and others in Latin, algebra, physiology, etc. A great need among the colored people is proper teachers, and we make a specialty of fitting young ladies and gentlemen for teaching, and in this direction the school has an enviable reputation.

During the past year there were seven members in the Theological class. The members of this department come to us with a very poor education, but earnestly desiring a better one. In the forenoon [they] attend to their recitations in the other departments. In the afternoon they meet me in Craig Hall or the library, where the studies are more especially directed to their ministerial work. The work here is a plain, simple, exegetical or explanatory reading of the Scriptures; also lessons in reading and speaking; lectures upon theology, dogmatic and practical; sermonizing, and other subjects of practical importance to the minister of the gospel. Twice each week a short sermon is delivered before the class by one of its members, after which the matter and manner are criticized by other members and lastly by myself. I have heard many poorer discourses from white ministers than some I have heard from them.

In our instruction in this department we aim to bring all the great fundamental teachings of the Scripture down to the capacity of the pupils, and the practical parts of the Bible to the ready grasp of their heretofore untutored minds. Our method of teaching and training is simple and practical. We aim that every member shall have at least a good English education until the higher branches are reached, and I would not have the colored conferences ordain any young man who does not possess this education.

The fourth annual session opens the 29th of October [1883] and continues for six months, with a vacation of one week between the Christmas holidays. Mrs. B.O. Maye, of Wingate, Indiana, will have charge of the primary department; Miss Jennie Watson, of Troy, Ohio, of the intermediate; Miss Belle Collum, of Dundee, New York, will teach in the classical or normal department. We have not yet secured our music teacher. Any of our friends from the North, or elsewhere, are cordially invited to visit us.

George Young continued as principal of the school for nine years. He was succeeded by the Rev. C.A. Beck, also of New York, who served for one year. Beck was followed by the Rev. J.F. Ullery, of Ohio, who was followed by the Rev. N. Del. McReynolds after one year. McReynolds came to the school in 1891 and served as principal (or president) for six years. In 1891 the corporate name of the school was changed to Franklinton Christian College. Under McReynolds' administration and that of his successor, the Rev. Z.A. Poste, of New York, the school made great progress. Its three buildings were completed and put in good condition. They were "on high ground, in a grove of beautiful oak trees which, with other favorable surroundings, made the location one of special attractiveness." All were well furnished.

Henry E. Long became president of the college in 1904 and served for thirteen years. He was the first of three Black presidents. In 1905 the Afro-Christian Conferences provided $1,000 for the purchase of a new site for the school. The new site was an eighty-three-acre tract of land located approximately one mile north of Franklinton, stretching one half mile along the Seaboard Airline Railroad and National Highway No. 1. Under Professor Long's administration gifts from the North came in and small amounts from the Black conferences of North Carolina and of Virginia for the erection of buildings on the new campus. One of these gifts made possible the purchase of a cement block-making machine. "Stones" for the new building were manufactured on the site, and gradually, a spacious, imposing three-story structure was built. A basement provided space for a kitchen, a dining room, a furnace room, store rooms, and a library. On the first floor were a large chapel, administrative offices, and classrooms. The second and third floors were partitioned at the center and provided dormitory space for male and for female students, the matron, and single teachers. Bishop's Cottage, home of the president, and three smaller cottages for staff families were soon added. The last building to be erected at Franklinton Christian College was never completed. It was a well-designed, two-story brick structure, with adequate kitchen, dining room, storage rooms, social rooms, and classrooms on the first floor. The second floor was to be the new dormitory for girls. The exterior and the roof were finished, and much of the material for completing the interior had been purchased and put in the building. However, the Great Depression halted construction, and for lack of funds the college closed in 1930.

Henry Long served longer and probably accomplished more than any other administrator of Franklinton Christian College. He was followed by the Rev. F.S. Hendershot, of Philadelphia, who served for three years. In 1920 the Rev. Smith A. Howell, pastor of Wesley Grove Christian Church, Newport News, Virginia, and president of the Afro-Christian Convention, became president of the college but served only two years for health reasons. The last president of the college was the Rev. James A. Henderson, who served as president of the school from 1922 until the school closed, in 1930. Henderson had graduated from the school in the class of 1901. He had taught in the public schools of North Carolina and at one time or another had held nearly every office in the North Carolina Colored Christian Conference. He was still pastor of three or four of its leading churches.

Franklinton Christian College was never a full-fledged college, but no institution had as great an influence upon the ministers and many of the lay leaders of the Black Christian churches. This becomes clear as we list a few of the graduates and students. *Ministers:* Smith A. Howell, John W. Meadows, James A. Henderson, Jiles B. Jones, John P. Mangrum, Jasper J. Holland, John W. Albright, Frederick A. Hargett, Richard D. Bullock, Jr., Charles A. Harris, J.J. Faulk, A.J. Holloway, Joseph H. Mann; *Laity:* Novella Hester (Reid), Max C. King (M.D.), Effie Sellars (Samuels) (Pettway), Mattie Hester (McCrimmon), James Christmas, Mary Edith Howell (Rainey), Susie I. Howell (Gregory), Florence Hester (Hargett), Eddie Lee Hargrove. Along with many others, these graduates and students of Franklinton Christian College ranked high among the outstanding ministers and lay leaders of the Black Christian church. The school instilled in its students deep religious convictions and motivation and gave an intellectual and spiritual vitality to those who became preachers, teachers, and doctors and to those who gave excellent guidance in their churches and communities. Two of its graduates returned to become college president.

President Smith A. Howell, in his biennial address at the 1916 session of the Afro-Christian Convention, stated:

The School house is the foe of ignorance whether in or out of the pulpit. . . . The rapid intellectual advancement of the pew is an imperative call for a trained ministry. Is the calling of the ministry of less dignity and importance than the call of such honorable professions as law, medicine, etc.? Possessing the opportunities so earnestly desired by our fathers, what justifying excuse is there for a lack of intellectual training on the part of the ministry of today? We are persuaded that our ministry is so well aware of these truths that no argument is needed to enforce the ammunition to scrutinize with care the candidates for admission to our conferences and insist on a high standard of qualifications. The future hope of our Church largely centers upon the School of Theology at Franklinton Christian College. This school is to be considered the Theological center from which goes a trained ministry. There is an imperative need that there be a thorough awakening to this truth. Our plea is for an educated ministry! An educated ministry!! An Educated Ministry!!! On this the respectability and influence of our Church depends.

Most of the Black ministers of the Christian Church who had any religious or theological training at all received that training at the Franklinton school. While the school gave literary training that was the equivalent of high school, its main educational thrust was simple, practical, biblical, religious and theological teachings.

This source of leadership for the Black Christian churches cannot be overemphasized. Franklinton Christian College provided ministerial training and indoctrination in the principles of the Christian denomination. Every minister trained at Franklinton knew the cardinal principles of the Christian church and had a practical working knowledge of the Bible and an evangelistic loyalty to the denomination. Whether in first grade or tenth grade, a student's religious training was basic and continuous during the years spent at Franklinton Christian College.

When the college closed in 1930 the main source of trained ministers for the Black Christian Church was cut off. With the merger of the Christian Church with the Congregational Churches, in 1931, all Congregational and Christian theological seminaries were open to Blacks who could qualify for admission. With few exceptions admission required full college training, and for years to come, in the Black Christian Church, aspirants to the ministry could rarely meet this requirement; nor were they ready for racially integrated, highly sophisticated theological training and study. This gulf still separates the Black Christian Church from the main body of its denomination.

The closing of Franklinton Christian College was the end of a dream. The printing press that had published *The Missionary Herald and Christian Star* (a journal of the Black Christian churches), Sunday school literature, college annuals, and minutes for the Afro-Christian Conferences and the Afro-Christian Convention was silenced. The sound of music no longer flowed from the buildings. The Max C. King Athletic Field was soon overgrown with weeds and was later planted to corn. Fodder was stored in the unfinished dormitory, and when this burned the steel girders were warped from the intense heat, windows and doors were destroyed, used and unused building materials were charred, and the roof was damaged beyond repair. The end of the college was cataclysmic for Black Christian churches. The college yell and the Franklinton College song, which expressed the high ideals and hopes of Franklinton Christian College, were no longer heard.

The College Yell

F.C.C.—F.C.C.—
She's all right—Yes sir-ee!
Rickity, Trickity, Sis-boom-bah!
Franklinton College, Rah! Rah!! Rah!!!

Franklinton College Song

Tune: "Maryland, My Maryland"

Dear College home, we sing to thee,
    Franklinton, our Franklinton;
We love thy halls, to us so free,
    Franklinton, our Franklinton;
Go where we may, our thoughts will dwell
Amid the scenes we love so well,
And of thy worth we'll gladly tell,
    Franklinton, our Franklinton.

Let others sing of ancient fame;
    Franklinton, our Franklinton;
Of storied halls and honored names,
    Franklinton, our Franklinton:

We feel thou art of nobler worth,
Though like our race, of humble birth;
Thy fame shall spread throughout the earth,
    Franklinton, our Franklinton.

Herein is taught God's sacred truth,
    Franklinton, our Franklinton;
A college home for age and youth,
    Franklinton, our Franklinton;
Here modern books and ancient lore
Are studied daily, o'er and o'er,
But Christ's own words are valued more,
    Franklinton, our Franklinton.

Forth from these halls shall go each year,
    Franklinton, our Franklinton;
Those who thine honored name shall wear,
    Franklinton, our Franklinton;
To spread, with knowledge, joy and peace
Among our own beloved race,
And make our land a better place,
    Franklinton, our Franklinton.

—D.E. Millard

Chapter 6

The Alfred E. Lawless Years

In 1914 the whole administrative pattern of AMA church work among Negroes in the South was changed. For forty years the work had been administered by secretaries or executives from the national or regional offices of the American Missionary Association. That year, however, Negro work in the South was reorganized into four districts.

—Alabama-Tennessee-Kentucky—the Rev. Harold M. Kingsley, superintendent

—Georgia-North and South Carolina—the Rev. Dallas J. Flynn, superintendent

—Louisiana-Mississippi-Arkansas—the Rev. Alfred E. Lawless, superintendent

—Texas-Oklahoma—the Rev. Malchus F. Foust, superintendent

Each of these districts had a district committee, which was usually made up of the superintendent and key leaders of groups of churches in the district. These key leaders met with the superintendent, planned action programs, and returned to initiate these programs among the ministers and churches of their group. These leaders also made regular reports to the district superintendent, who, in turn, reported to the executives of the American Missionary Association. This plan of organization and administration of the Negro work in the South was in operation from 1914 through 1919.

It should be noted that this period included the years of World War I and the early aftermath of that war. The changes— both natural and man-made—that took place in the South during this time and in the following decade were little short of revolutionary. The coming of the boll weevil, the army worm, the Mexican bean beetle; resulting crop failures; the collapse of cotton tenancy; war conscriptions and rationing of food and of other living essentials all contributed to near financial and economic chaos in the agricultural South, especially for Negroes and poor whites. The ensuing migrations from vast rural areas to industrialized urban centers in the South and from south to north meant not only the shifting of populations but also the redistribution and intensification of problems of race, housing, and social and occupational adjustments.

When this new plan of administration was begun, in 1914, there were 165 Black Congregational churches, mostly small, in eleven states of the Old South. Less than twenty-five of these churches had memberships that exceeded 100. The 164 churches had a total membership of 10,487. The congregations were poor, as evidenced by their contribution of less than $5,000 per year to the support of denominational benevolences. Home expenses of $39,640 were not for a single church but for a large portion of the 164 that reported home expenses. The passionate zeal of AMA ministers and teachers and their Black disciples and their compassion for the underprivileged enabled them to carry the gospel, to establish little churches, and to bring enlightenment to many of the most benighted areas of the South. The following chart shows the distribution of Black Congregational churches, according to states, in 1914.

The amount listed for denominational benevolences in each case is reasonably accurate, as these figures are verified by the national office. The home expense figure, however, shows what was reported by the churches. A number of churches did not report home expenses, and many that did included the pastor's salary in this amount. Also, several states gave more to local benevolences than to denominational apportionment. Perhaps this could be justified on the basis of dire local need. It is also noteworthy that at the 69th (1915) annual meeting of the American Missionary Association the report on church work among Negroes differed somewhat from the above figures. There were 175 churches, 94 "ministers and missionaries," 10,233 church members, and 8,740 Sunday school scholars. Benevolent contributions were set at $3,224. The amount raised for local church purposes was $48,931. The report continues:

Additions to the churches constitute an advance of 232 (members) upon the previous year. . . . Nearly 1,400 new

76

State	Churches	Members	Ministers	Gifts	Home Expenses
Alabama	20	1,587	22	$1,461	$7,934
Arkansas	1	115	1	0	420
Georgia	26	2,143	19	414	5,505
Kentucky	2	280	2	26	1,440
Louisiana	31	1,691	20	1,395	9,950
Mississippi	5	270	4	206	345
North Carolina	56	2,523	27	976	6,824
Oklahoma	3	154	3	36	1,042
South Carolina	7	380	3	20	1,220
Tennessee	5	1,063	5	98	2,001
Texas	9	281	5	101	2,959
Totals	165	10,487	111	$4,733	$39,640

Sunday School scholars are reported, and in spite of the hard times there is an advance in the benevolent contributions, though a slight decrease in amount raised for self support.

In its details, the work of the Negro churches has been unusually interesting and efficient. . . . The field superintendents appointed a year ago have amply justified their election. The fruits of their work are evidenced by a hopeful spirit everywhere, by an unusually enthusiastic series of local and state conference meetings, and by special institutes for ministers. More systematic investigation is now possible as to the needs of the field, resources of the fields, as well as more careful study given to current church problems.

At the time of this change in the administrative process the Black Congregational churches of the South, especially town and country churches, were already in serious trouble. Recession was offset temporarily by the enthusiastic and efficient leadership of the field superintendents. They stayed close to the churches and their ministers; organized ministers' institutes; developed indigenous programs of evangelism, religious education, youth work, and women's work in the churches and in the conferences and associations. When the United States entered World War I, migration accelerated. Invasion of the boll weevil, floods, and crop failures across the South caused this migratory movement to accelerate to alarming proportions.

In March of 1917 a special Pastors' Institute and Farmers' Conference was held at Talladega College, which brought together over 250 representatives from several southern states. A number of prominent white citizens were also present. The purpose of this meeting was "to consider the problems of the Rural Church, and to inquire into the cause for the unrest and migration of so many Negroes to Northern states." Near the close of the meeting the body adopted, unanimously, "Declarations" that clearly pointed up reasons for widespread unrest and dissatisfaction among Negroes generally:

—Failure of crops due to floods, frost, and the visitation of the boll weevil; difficulty, amounting many times to impossibility, in securing the needed advances, in some cases even to a sack of flour, to the farmer class

—Attitudes of many planters toward their tenants in not providing housing suitable for human habitation

—Poor schools, small salaries for teachers, and uncomfortable buildings

That newspapers and prominent persons refrain from unkind and untrue statements which tend to arouse prejudices against a struggling for a better life. (Judge Abernathy's recent speech or newspaper article in Birmingham is a sample of such utterances.)

That public officials grant such a division of the public school funds that our children may enjoy equal advantages with the whites.

That the practice of lynching receive general condemnation, and that any Negro accused of criminal offenses be guaranteed an impartial trial by an organized court.

That there be a recognition of the needs of our people for general social betterment, improved housing conditions; and especially that the tenant class on the farms be provided with dwellings fit for human occupation.

Such declarations delineated the problems, but the white South was not ready to listen, and the migrations and the lynchings continued. The effect on many rural churches in the South was devastating. Except in a few areas of high incidence of Black ownership of homesites and land, whole communities were stripped of Blacks who were in their active years, who sought employment, decent wages, and a better life in the North. This meant the depletion of rural church membership and the death of any hope for the future. The day has come when the only rural Congregational churches that remain among Blacks in the South are in communities where a high percentage of Black people owned and still own real property. It is hardly less than miraculous that those first field superintendents, through persistent zeal and widespread evangelism, were able to hold these Black Congregational churches together. There was some increase in financial support of the local churches and of denominational apportionment. There was a remarkable growth in the total membership. It should be noted, however, that many churches (mostly rural) made no reports for the *Year Book;* the figures given were for a previous year. Approximately one fifth of the members reported were absentee members who, presumably, had migrated to northern cities.

The field superintendents spearheaded nearly every significant event and accomplishment in the area. They were ably assisted and supported by such notable leaders as James Brown, Anniston, Alabama; J.C. Olden, Birmingham, Alabama; H.H. Proctor, Atlanta, Georgia; W.L. Cash Sr., Savannah, Georgia; H.H. Dunn, New Orleans, Louisiana; E.G. Harris, Louisville, Kentucky; Perfect R. DeBerry, Raleigh, North Carolina; Arthur F. Almes, Wilmington, North Carolina; A.L. DeMond, Charleston, South Carolina; and Russell S. Brown, Memphis, Tennessee. In 1918 the National Convention of Congregational Workers Among Negroes held its biennial meeting at Raleigh, North Carolina, at First Congregational Church; the Rev. Perfect R. DeBerry was the minister of that church. At the same time, an American Missionary Association teachers' institute brought to Raleigh a "goodly gathering" of association secretaries, teachers, and new recruits. The convention was attended by ministers and delegates from all parts of the South, as well as a few from northern cities where Black Congregational churches had been or were being established. It was at this meeting that Dr. and Mrs. Henry Curtis McDowell (Bessie Fonville) were commissioned as American Board Missionaries to Angola, West Africa. Of this incident Clara M. Standish, then English teacher at Talladega College, wrote the following:

One of the most thrilling hours of the Convention was the service commissioning Rev. and Mrs. H.C. McDowell. . . . Dr. C.H. Patton spoke most eloquently on the dire needs of Africa, and called the going of these young American Negroes back to the Motherland the return of the African Pilgrims whose involuntary coming to America antedated by one year the coming of the Mayflower Pilgrims.

Both Mr. and Mrs. McDowell are Talladega graduates of the Class of 1917. After the singing of that grand old Negro Spiritual, "I know the Lord has laid his hands on me," Mr. McDowell responded feelingly, saying that since he had been called to the ministry at all, he felt called to the neediest place. The colored Congregationalists of the

South are already developing a deeper interest in foreign missions, since they are to have a mission station manned by people of their own race and supported by their own contributions.

It was at this meeting that the leaders of Black Congregational churches pledged their support to the McDowells and to the Galangue Station, which they later established in Portuguese West Africa. For many years to come Angola was the watchword in every conference and convention meeting and in every women's missionary society of the Black churches. Although the support given was never adequate, no missionary work of the American Board was more colorful or effectively carried on, and no American Board missionaries received better support or more enthusiastic commendation than did the McDowells.

The National Convention of Congregational Workers Among Colored People was at its highest level of achievement at its 1924 meeting in Chattanooga, Tennessee. The same is probably true of Congregationalism among Black people in the South. What the convention accomplished at this meeting for the Galangue Station in Angola, West Africa brought this station to the forefront of foreign missionary work of the denomination. The ministers and churches represented in the meeting pledged themselves to search for a doctor for Galangue, to build a school with auditorium suitable for multiple use, to build a nursery and dormitories; and to underwrite the Galangue Station for $20,000.00 per year. Sam and Bertha Coles were already in Galangue. The McDowells attended the meeting with their sons, Curtis and Elmer Hugh. Elmer *Hugh* was baptized at this meeting by Dr. Henry *Hugh* Proctor. (See insert for picture of people who attended the convention.)

Churches and individuals were inspired; and although the Depression changed everything, by 1929, Dr. Aaron McMillan had been appointed and was on his way to Galangue; an adequate school with auditorium had been built; nursery and dormitories had been built; and a permanent missionary residence was already occupied. Galangue Clubs sprang up in a number of churches. Under the leadership of E.H. Phillips, the Young People's Summer Conference in Louisiana financed the residence; Plymouth Church of Washington, D.C. gave one of the dormitories; a woman in New Orleans gave the nursery; a layman had a model T Ford delivered to Galangue at his personal expense; and among all Black Congregational churches there was genuine commitment to the Galangue Mission Project. The ministers and lay leaders who attended the 1924 meeting of the convention not only spearheaded the Galangue Mission Project, but gave outstanding leadership in Black Congregational churches in the South, and in establishing churches for Black Congregationalists who had migrated to northern communities.

In 1918 the field superintendents adopted the denominational program to enlist a million Congregationalists during October and November in a "simultaneous study of the world's desperate needs and how they should be met" and through a simultaneous every-member canvass on Sunday, December 8 to raise "16 million dollars as part of our share in meeting these needs—4 millions for missions and charity and 12 millions for Local Church support." A directory of the churches was published, and although only seven churches had met their 1917 goals, the 1918 goals were announced. This plan of promotion and of intensive cultivation of the churches made it possible, during the war years and for nearly a decade following, for Black Congregational churches of the South, despite their poverty and their losses, to do better than the national percentage averages of the denomination in church membership and in church school enrollment, and in financial support of missions and home expenses. This form of administration was continued until 1919.

The moving spirit in the process was Alfred E. Lawless. Born in the little town of Thibodaux, Louisiana on July 16, 1873, he attended Straight College (now Dillard University) in New Orleans, from which he received the B.A. degree in 1902 and the B.D. degree in 1904. He founded Beecher Memorial Church of New Orleans in 1904 and continued to pastor this church until 1910. For one year (1904–5) he also served as pastor of University Church in New Orleans. In 1910 he resigned as pastor of Beecher Church to become full-time minister of University Church at Straight College, which he served until 1914. During all these pastoral years he was statistical secretary of the Louisiana State Conference of Congregational Churches.

After serving as field superintendent for five years, in 1919 Lawless was chosen superintendent of Negro church work in the South, and his residence and office were moved from New Orleans to Atlanta, Georgia.

At this time, several pastors followed their members' lead and migrated to the North, where they either served or organized Black Congregational churches: H.H. Proctor to Brooklyn, New York; Sidney O.B. Johnson to Buffalo, New York; James C. Olden and Arthur F. Almes to Washington, D.C.; Samuel L. Laviscount to Boston; Russell S. Brown to Cleveland; and Charles W. Burton and Harold M. Kingsley to Chicago.

Statistics show something of the struggles that Congregational churches, both Black and white, were having to keep open and to keep supplied with pastoral leadership. By 1919 only 152 Black churches were listed, and at least thirty-eight of these had no pastor; many others had preaching services only one or two Sundays a month. The reported total membership of 9,531 was probably optimistic, since membership figures for many churches had been picked up from previous records. There is no doubt that the decline of Congregational church work among Black people of the South had set in.

Even though Alfred Lawless was an intelligent administrator, a good organizer, an excellent preacher and speaker, an untiring worker, and a person of impeccable character, from the outset, as general superintendent, he faced difficult and challenging problems. He was envied by some who had not been promoted. When income for the national boards fell off drastically and cuts had to be made across the board, Lawless had the unlovely task of making adjustments and of informing the ministers of reductions in their salaries and in other appropriations to Negro church work in the South. In his report at the annual meeting of the American Missionary Association, in Detroit, Michigan, November 8, 1922, he spoke of his dilemma.

It is generally admitted that a Negro who succeeds a white administrator in any capacity among his own race faces a very delicate and trying experience. In this case the promotion of a District Superintendent over his former associates added to the delicacy of the situation. Problems growing out of this adjustment occupied much of the thought of the Superintendent during the first year of his work. The second year was marked by a general feeling of uncertainty due to the absence of a permanent Corresponding Secretary in the Missions Department. The third year began with a full quota of District Superintendents and the friendly attitude of the new Secretary [Dr. Fred L. Brownlee].

Some problems were inherent. Lawless' area of visitatic was several times greater than it had been, and travel conveniences and comforts were extremely limited, especially in rural areas and more especially for Negroes. Each district had its own peculiar types of people and problems: Louisiana with its "Creole population of excitable temperaments"; Texas with its "proud, self-assertive Negroes"; Alabama-Tennessee-Kentucky with their "more intelligent, yet more conservative and cautious people"; North Carolina with its "non-progressive highlander folk"; and the great variety of Black cultures ranging from the urbanized Atlantans to the natives of the coastal regions of Georgia and the Carolinas. While district superintendents usually dealt with only one set of peculiar problems, the general superintendent was caught up with all of them.

There were unavoidable changes in personnel. Harold M. Kingsley was chosen superintendent of Negro church work in the North; Henry S. Barnwell, with headquarters in Montgomery, Alabama, became field superintendent of the Alabama-Tennessee-Kentucky district in his stead. Dallas J. Flynn developed a strong enthusiasm for evangelistic work and moved on his own into full-time work as an evangelist; George J. Thomas succeeded him as field superintendent of the district of Georgia and the Carolinas. Edward H. Phillips, who had had a long association with Lawless at Beecher Church and had shown keen interest and efficiency in Sunday school work, youth activities, recreation for children, and scouting, both in the church and in the city, upon Lawless' recommendation, was employed by the Congregational Sunday School Extension Society as full-time church school worker for the combined Louisiana-Texas district. Malchus F. Foust resigned as field superintendent and became pastor of churches in San Antonio and in Runge, Texas.

Henderson H. Dunn became field superintendent of the combined Louisiana-Texas district.

With this slightly enlarged field staff and with wide awake, forward-looking young ministers filling pastorates that had been left vacant by those who had moved to northern cities, Lawless sought to stimulate church life in both urban and rural centers. Ministerial institutes for the purpose of "enriching and inspiring the lives of the pastors" were held at strategic points in each district. In these institutes modern church methods, a modern interpretation of the teachings of Jesus, the meaning and requirements of Christian stewardship and evangelism as a means to enlarging church membership and extending the church into neglected areas were stressed. Organized women's work in each church was emphasized. A special effort was made to develop a definite program of religious education, with trained leadership, that would try to explore and meet the needs of each individual church. This program was to provide "a larger place for helpful activities, and involvement on the part of young people in the church and community program."

Vacation Bible schools among Black churches were started in the summer of 1924. Four Black young people were commissioned by the Congregational Sunday School Extension Society as summer workers. James A. Herod worked in Beaumont and Port Arthur, Texas. Edwin L. Phillips was assigned to Louisiana and spent the summer at Opelousas, Abbeville, Gueydan, New Iberia, and Morbihan (Kamp Knighton), Louisiana. Elvis W. Spearman went to Tallahassee, Florida and worked there and at Beachton and Thomasville, Georgia. Kathryn M. Turrentine (who was to become my wife) served at churches and community centers in her native state of Alabama, at Sheffield, Muscle Shoals, Florence, Ensley, Anniston, and Bexar.

The slogan for these student summer workers was "Using my life where it counts for the most." They pioneered a new approach in Christian education and church extension, with a primary concern for training children and young people. The vacation Bible school was a must at nearly every point visited. In addition, these workers "did what their hands found to do." They organized or reorganized youth work in many churches, started social clubs, developed recreational programs, conducted Bible classes for adults, visited the sick, and frequently supplied pulpits, "not as preachers but as Christian workers among the people." They also helped to establish and worked in young people's summer conferences at Kamp Knighton, Louisiana and Kings Mountain, North Carolina. New playgrounds with tennis courts were developed at Beaumont, Texas and at Thomasville, Georgia. New mission Sunday schools were started at Rynella, Louisiana and at a location twelve miles out from Bexar, Alabama. Four student summer service workers had "used their lives where they counted for the most" and had spearheaded a new emphasis on religious education and youth work among the Black churches of the South.

This emphasis was accelerated in the development of young people's summer conferences, ministers' and lay leaders' conferences, and training institutes for an increasing number of student summer service workers. It was in such conferences and institutes that many ministerial students received their first field experiences in pastoral ministry, preaching, and religious training of children and young people. Several young women who entered this program became full-time religious workers. After teaching a year at Gloucester Institute, Capahoosic, Virginia, Kathryn Turrentine, the first Negro woman in student summer service, was commissioned as an extension worker. She was "the first young woman to be appointed for Extension Service among the colored churches of the South." Although she was stationed first in Raleigh to work among Black churches in the Carolinas, her parish was soon extended across the entire Southeast, and she moved to Atlanta for closer association with Superintendent Lawless and for closer coordination of the work among Black Congregational churches of the South. While in Atlanta she lived in the Lawless home. Even though Dr. Lawless was already weakened by his first paralytic stroke, he drove himself beyond his strength to enlarge the work of the churches, to establish new centers of religious training, and to give constructive leadership and counsel to ministers and lay leaders across the South. Despite the fact that he had the best medical service that could be provided and the constant care of a courageous, loyal wife, he was never a well man again. But his spirit never flagged. His deep personal concern and his dreams for the enlargement of Congregational church work among Negroes in the South fired the imagination of his co-workers with directives and objectives to be sought. What he desired to accomplish and could not was often brought to full fruit by his wife, Harriet; Kathryn Turrentine, the extension worker; Madeline White, loyal and efficient office secretary; and by many faithful ministers and leaders.

I came back to the South as pastor of the Howard Church in Nashville, Tennessee in July 1925. It was my privilege to meet Dr. Alfred Lawless, Harriet Dunn Lawless, and Kathryn Turrentine as a team at the Tennessee-Kentucky Conference at Plymouth Church in Louisville, Kentucky in May 1926. Also present at this meeting were the district superintendent, Henry S. Barnwell; secretary of the American Missionary Association, Fred L. Brownlee; the alumni secretary of American Missionary Association colleges, George N. White (brother of Madeline White of the Atlanta office); and the Rev. William J. Turrentine, who was soon to be my father-in-law. I saw Dr. Lawless only a few times after that, but I came to know him and the quality of his life and his ministry best through my wife's account of her association with Dr. and Mrs. Lawless and their three children: Gertrude Lawless Martin, teacher and resident of Chicago, Illinois; Prof. Oscar Lawless, Talladega College, Talladega, Alabama; and Dr. Theodore K. Lawless, internationally renowned dermatologist. I had the privilege of visiting in the Lawless homes in Atlanta and in Chicago, and Oscar had been a delightful guest in our home in Dudley, North Carolina. The Lawlesses were a great Congregational family. None made greater contributions to Black Congregational churches in the South and to our denomination and its institutions, both in service and in material means, than did this family.

I witnessed many of the changes that took place among the Black Congregational churches of the South from 1925 through 1931. The worst American depression reached its climax during these years. The migrations continued to weaken beyond recovery many small churches. Due to lack of income the American Missionary Association was forced to make drastic cuts in all its appropriations to institutions, including church work among Negroes in the South. District superintendents' offices were closed. As the health of Dr. Lawless continued to decline, Henry S. Barnwell was promoted successively to acting superintendent and then to superintendent of Negro church work. H.H. Dunn and George J. Thomas had returned to pastoral work. A few churches were vitalized by the introduction of social service programs that provided kindergartens, child care centers, playgrounds, and so on, which justified financial support both from the American Missionary Association and from the communities in which these centers were located. Still, the validity of the American Missionary Association church work among Negroes was being seriously questioned.

Perhaps the greatest change in Negro church work in the South came with the merger of the Congregational and Christian churches, in 1931. Alfred Lawless lived through these turbulent years. Although he was physically an invalid, he never lost his intense interest in the work. He attended the 1926 meeting of the National Convention of Congregational Workers Among Negroes, in Detroit, Michigan. With considerable difficulty, he addressed the meeting, showing keen insight into the plight of the Black churches and giving wise counsel to the delegation. The last time I saw him—three summers later, at the Kings Mountain Summer Conference—he was much weaker and speech was nearly impossible. He sat quietly and attentively through most of the sessions. His wife was at his side constantly.

Alfred Lawless died in Atlanta, Georgia on September 9, 1933. He, his wife, and their two sons now rest in Mount Olivet Cemetery, a short distance from the main entrance to Dillard University. They gave much of themselves to Congregationalism, to Beecher Church, and to Dillard (Straight College); these institutions meant a great deal to them.

Chapter 7

The Henry S. Barnwell Years

Henry Stephen Barnwell, born August 1, 1881, was a native of Charleston, South Carolina. Charleston Negroes had many cultural advantages. A high percentage were mulattoes. Many were given their freedom before the outbreak of the Civil War; a number had learned to read and write. The leading builders, metalworkers, and artisans of the city were Negroes. A teacher at Avery Institute wrote that the whiteness, the intelligence, and the bearing of her students compared most favorably with that of the children of New England.

Henry S. Barnwell grew up in Charleston and received all his training through high school at Avery Institute, completing his studies there in 1899. He did college and seminary work at Talladega College and graduated with the class of 1903. On January 20, 1904 he was ordained to the Congregational ministry at his home church in Charleston. His first pastorate was the College Church, Talladega. After three years at Talladega, he continued his pastoral work—six years at Lake Charles, Louisiana and five years at Thomasville, Georgia. When he was ready to leave Thomasville, Richard Williams, an officer in the Thomasville church, wrote:

Rev. H.S. Barnwell has tendered his resignation as pastor of Bethany Congregational Church to take up work in another field. We wish to express to him and to the A.M.A., under whose direction he is acting, our deepest regret at the turn of affairs which takes him from us.

He has endeared himself not only to the members of Bethany Church, but to the entire community by his large heart, his impartial service, and his whole-hearted interest in any and everything which concerns our people. . . .

The Church Building will stand as a monument to his great optimism and never-failing trust in Him whom he served. In the face of discouragements and seemingly impossible barriers, he labored on cheerfully and hopefully until the work was brought to a successful close.

We shall also miss Mrs. Barnwell, who entered so heartily into the Church and community life, showing the true spirit of service. Although we shall miss them sorely, we bid them Godspeed in their new field and follow them with our prayers, that the greatest measure of success may attend their efforts, as we feel they so richly deserve.

By vote of the church this letter, dated March 15, 1915, became part of the permanent records of the church, and copies were sent to Barnwell and to the secretary of the American Missionary Association.

From Thomasville, Barnwell moved to Florida, where he served as principal of Fessenden Academy, under the auspices of the American Missionary Association. In 1921 he returned to church work as district superintendent of Black Congregational churches in Alabama, Kentucky, and Tennessee. He was doubtless the most aggressive and the most promising of the district leaders, so that when Alfred Lawless became ill, he was called to Atlanta to become his assistant, moving gradually into full responsibility as superintendent of all Negro Congregational churches in the South. He served in the latter position from 1921 to March 1, 1942. During most of these years great changes were taking place and Black church work in the South was in serious difficulty.

One of the most significant changes was brought about by a survey of Black churches receiving financial aid from the American Missionary Association. On September 14, 1926 the executive committee of the association voted to engage William A. Daniel "to make a careful study of all the Southern churches to which the A.M.A. is granting aid." Seventy-five churches were studied, sixty-three of which were receiving aid toward their ministers' salaries. The other twelve were receiving aid toward their social service programs. Daniel spent approximately a year making this study and compiling his report.

The results of the Daniel Report were revealed at the 1928 annual meeting of the American Missionary Association; the implications were clear. Superintendent Barnwell made a desperate defense of the churches:

Viewing the diminishing numbers of Congregational churches among Negroes of the South, someone may ask, "Has it paid?" If numbers alone are considered, the answer is unquestionably, "No"; but if spiritual values are in the equation, we unhesitatingly answer, "Yes!" The exodus of Southern Negroes which started some years ago has not yet ceased. This constant drain robbed Southern churches, not only of many cultured families but took away also a number of outstanding leaders and ministers. Should we call the roll of the latter class, we would include DeBerry, Garner, Proctor, Kingsley, Brown, Johnson and others who got their starts in the South. This fine type of Christian cannot be measured by numbers or rated by dollars.

But what of the group of little churches still remaining? Do they really justify their existence? Are they at all indigenous? What is the hope of self-sustenance and permanent stability? Many fine examples might be given in answer to these queries, but time permits but one illustration.

A glowing description of the pastoral work and social service program being carried on by George J. Thomas and his staff in Winston-Salem, North Carolina followed. He concluded:

To any who may still wonder about the use of assisting Congregational churches among Negroes in the South a final word might be added. Some ten years ago a product of Talladega College, Henry Curtis McDowell, was selected by the American Board as its representative to found a mission in Angola, West Africa. The beginning of this enterprise meant the raising of some $2,000.00 by the Southern churches. The record shows that more than $3,000.00 were raised the first year. Advancing years not only prove that Angola is now a splendid success, but that colored churches have made it one of the outstanding missionary projects of Congregationalism. Furthermore, the churches of the South contributed in 1927 more than $6,500.00 to world wide missions.

Copies of the report were sent to concerned persons of the administrative committee and to all members of a special committee that had been appointed. After this special committee met with Fred L. Brownlee, American Missionary Association secretary, and with William Daniel, Superintendent Barnwell and his assistant, the Rev. Norman A. Holmes, were called in to give their reactions to the survey. "Then the special committee invited Messrs. William L. Cash of New Orleans; E.C. Lawrence of Birmingham; W.J. King of Lexington, Kentucky; C.S. Ledbetter of Charleston, South Carolina; H.H. Proctor of Brooklyn, New York, and H.M. Kingsley of Chicago to sit in an advisory council at which the recommendations contained in the Survey were thoroughly discussed."

The Daniel Report recommended that aid to ten of the seventy-five churches should be discontinued immediately; eight should be put on a trial basis, giving them the benefit of the doubt until the situations became clear-cut; sixteen should be continued on a missionary basis, as churches "that serve a true missionary purpose as that term is generally understood"; twenty-nine churches should be developed into self-supporting churches.

The special committee, augmented by the co-opted persons named above, finally agreed that all aided projects should be closely supervised and encouraged by the Atlanta office, and that certain criteria, requirements, and policies in administration should apply in all instances where financial aid is given. The purpose of the Daniel survey was to discover the true condition of Black Congregational churches in the South and to recommend procedures by which the American Missionary Association could help these churches to become self-supporting. There was considerable discussion. Following is a summary of the ten recommendations adopted by the committee.

    1. That the American Missionary Association should cooperate with the Atlanta office "in the selection of only well qualified men who are willing to work" toward the goal of moving the church to full self-support.

    2. That the terms on which aid would be granted should be determined by facts that indicated the possibility of steady growth and the development of a well-ordered, serviceable, and influential church.

    3. That an aided church should be required to furnish the Atlanta office an official list of its membership and

periodic information on the condition of buildings and facilities, the services and activities of pastor and church; and the financial condition of the church; and that the Atlanta office should prepare an annual statement of the "upward or downward trends in each church, with recommendations."

4. That each church and pastor should enter into an agreement with the AMA that the church would progress toward self-support in a stated number of years, aid being reduced annually and the church assuming a larger portion of salary each year. If the church defaulted on the agreement, aid would be discontinued after one year.

5. That the appointment of members of the administrative staff of Negro church work in the South should be approved by the administrative committee of the AMA and that a standing committee on church appropriations should be chosen annually by the administrative committee.

The implementation of these recommendations was primarily the task of the Atlanta office and of the pastors of aided churches. Required reports were time-consuming for all concerned and on-the-spot scrutiny of projects was offensive to most. A report prepared by the Atlanta office for the years 1929-33 covered eighty-four churches but did not include any churches in South Carolina, Tennessee, or Texas. Thirty-four of these churches were receiving aid toward their pastors' salaries during all or part of this five-year period. Three others were receiving aid toward social service programs. Total membership of the eighty-four churches showed a neglible increase of only forty-two. The apportionment (missions) giving dropped from $3,827 to $1,672—an alarming decrease of 56 percent. The Great Depression was at least partly responsible for this decline, as well as for the extreme difficulty of securing and retaining well-qualified, youthful pastors in these aided situations. In every instance where such leadership was obtained, there was progress in expansion of program, increase of membership, and in financial support of the local church and of denominational needs. In most cases where old pastors were retained (and there were few other choices for them or the churches) the opposite was true. A grave and continuing problem for the Black Congregational Christian churches of the South was that of training or attracting, supporting and continuing in the work young, committed, well-qualified pastors. Thus, the Daniel survey and recommendations set up many aided Black churches and their ministers for this treatment at a time when they most needed aid.

The merger of Congregational and Christian churches, in 1931, enlarged the geographical area of administration by adding Virginia and a small group of Afro-Christian churches, listed as the New York, New Jersey, and Pennsylvania Conference, which nearly tripled the number of Black churches to be administered. The merger presented other aggravating problems. Between Black Christians and Black Congregationalists there were wide differences in cultural and in worship patterns; in the training level of ministers; in the organization and general administration (or lack of it) of the churches. The transfer of Negro church work in 1936 from the American Missionary Association to the extension division of the Board of Home Missions freed the American Missionary Association division to major in education and in unique types of community service programs, such as the Bricks Rural Life Center at Bricks, North Carolina. But the superintendent of Negro church work had to learn a whole new set of rules in adjustment from American Missionary Association policies to extension division policies, which was no small task.

As a result of the merger, the center of the Negro church population moved to North Carolina-Virginia—the stronghold of the predominantly Afro-Christian churches—and that population became predominantly rural and Afro-Christian. All these combined to catapult the superintendent of Negro church work into an impossible situation, with no precedent for dealing with many of the problems.

The situation was aggravated still further. In September 1927 Alfred E. Lawless finally retired from all administrative responsibility; Kathryn M. Turrentine was married on September 15 of that year and became mistress of the manse of Howard Church in Nashville, Tennessee; Madeline White, office secretary (and sister of Walter White of NAACP fame and of George White, American Missionary Association alumni secretary), resigned to seek a salary commensurate with her office efficiency.

The Rev. Norman A. Holmes had already come from a short pastorate at First Church of Savannah, Georgia to serve as associate to Henry Barnwell, but the above resignations forced the Atlanta office into a series of attempts to replace the extension worker and the office secretary. These attempts were seriously hampered by the inability of the superintendent to offer adequate salaries.

Kathryn Turrentine Stanley was followed in extension service, first by Louise R. McKinney—who, after two years, turned to teaching in Presbyterian schools as a way out—and then by Eleanor Heithe, who became the wife of the Rev. Charles F. Rush, pastor of New Emmanuel Church of Charlotte, North Carolina. Phoebe Fraser Morgan, later known only as Phoebe Fraser, started off as office secretary and played a major role in composing and setting up copy for the *Southern News* (later *The Amistad*), conference paper for Negro church work in the South. When Eleanor Heithe married, Phoebe Fraser succeeded her as the director of religious education and continued in this position until Henry Barnwell died and his successor began work, October 1, 1942.

Reference has already been made to the Daniel Report, to Daniel's recommendations regarding the seventy-five churches surveyed, and to the effects of these recommendations upon Negro church work in the South. One notable effect of the survey was that it revealed the true state of a number of aided churches. They were alive mainly because of the aid that their pastors received. The survey made it necessary for the American Missionary Association to reexamine its entire approach to church work among Negroes. At the winter meeting of the American Missionary Association (1928), Barnwell and his staff reported that

the year 1928 differed little, statistically considered, from 1927. The churches just about held their own, with the Louisiana churches doing exceptionally well. The year was a period of transition with a new A.M.A. policy in the making. Therefore, we turn optimistically to the days ahead.

95

Not more churches but better churches is to be our guiding principle of our Southern Church Work for the next few years. This principle becomes primary as a result of a most timely evolution in the Southern Church Work. . . .

With the facts in the open [the Daniel survey], "Aunt Mary Ann" handed in her resignation of *Patron* of the Southern Church Work and accepted the challenge of the survey to become the *Big-Friend.* As such, she plans to help the churches to become self-supporting, self-respecting centers for individual improvement and community betterment.

Despite the excellent planning and the untiring work of the staff, statistics through the Barnwell years show that the trend in important areas of Black Congregational churches in the South continued to be downward.

The above statistics were taken from Congregational or Congregational Christian year books for the years indicated. Admittedly, these statistics, like most statistics, may have many discrepancies. Each year some of the figures were lifted from a previous year's report or year book. Some of the data concerning memberships and church finances were estimates of the pastor or of some church officer, usually the church clerk. In each instance, amounts given for denominational missions are accurate; these figures were furnished or verified by the receiving boards and agencies of the denomination. However, these are the best statistics available, and because each year the degree of inconsistency was about the same, the information is reasonably dependable. The tables show the trends in the projected life and action of the Black churches in the South.

In 1938 I was given a small travel allowance and was asked to gather, by personal contact, statistics of the Afro-Christian churches of North Carolina and of Virginia. I visited each conference and picked up copies of minutes of previous conference sessions. I also called on a majority of the local churches, often accompanied by the pastor. We chatted with church clerks and other officers, scanned record books, if any, and made extensive notes on matters of relative value. This study uncovered very few changes in the facts about the Afro-Christian churches that

Southern Black Congregational Churches Only—1928
(Before 1931 Congregational Christian Merger)

Conferences or States	No. Chs.	Memberships	S.S. Scholars	Benevolences OCWM	Benevolences Other	Home Expenses	Property Values
Ala.-Miss.	20	1,044	1,776	$1,462	$ 365	$ 14,263	$ 71,150
Ga.-S.C.	22	1,756	1,181	1,176	920	18,785	357,900
Louisiana	17	917	706	932	856	17,629	154,350
N.C.	47	2,476	1,972	598	1,468	26,470	271,200
Tenn.-Ky.	9	1,229	820	434	383	22,157	306,000
Texas-Okla.	13	546	506	354	266	15,301	159,350
Totals	128	7,968	6,961	$4,956	$4,258	$114,605	$1,319,950

Black Congregational Christian Churches—1933
(After the Merger)

Conferences or States	No. Chs.	Memberships	S.S. Scholars	Benevolences OCWM	Other	Home Expenses	Property Values
Ala.-Miss.	17	766	528	$ 828	$ 108	$ 5,673	$ 132,980
Ga.-S.C.	18	1,495	643	927	438	11,910	283,646
Louisiana	17	1,114	786	494	419	10,264	158,201
N.C. Chr.	92	7,837	2,654	53	0	2,125	223,200
N.C. Cong'l.	45	2,170	1,604	399	105	19,115	275,400
Tenn.-Ky.	8	1,367	378	317	348	11,038	369,500
Texas-Okla.	12	434	394	266	266	11,044	141,650
Va. Chr.	31	2,386	616	128	154	2,115	112,475
Totals	240	17,569	7,603	$3,412	$1,838	$73,284	$1,697,052
Chr. Only	123	10,223	3,270	$ 181	$ 154	$ 4,240	$ 335,675
Cong'l Only	117	7,346	4,333	$3,231	$1,684	$69,044	$1,361,377

Black Congregational Christian Churches—1938

Conferences or States	No. Chs.	Memberships	S.S. Scholars	Benevolences OCWM	Benevolences Other	Home Expenses	Property Values
Ala.-Miss.	16	827	623	$ 647	$ 108	$ 6,608	$ 179,600
Ga.-S.C.	13	1,219	546	469	0	3,633	283,446
Louisiana	14	955	501	111	559	12,703	81,225
N.C. Chr.	101	10,568	4,668	29	1,265	15,329	307,975
N.C. Cong'l	42	1,911	1,885	413	456	23,796	252,200
Tenn.-Ky.	8	1,153	467	371	358	7,672	291,500
Texas-Okla.	13	423	327	199	189	8,745	101,600
Va. Chr.	32	2,913	1,216	135	318	7,947	117,500
Totals	239	19,969	10,233	$2,374	$3,253	$86,433	$1,615,046
Chr. Only	133	13,481	5,884	$ 164	$1,583	$23,276	$ 425,475
Cong'l Only	106	6,488	4,349	$2,210	$1,670	$63,157	$1,189,571

Black Congregational Christian Churches—1943

Conferences or States	No. Chs.	Memberships	S.S. Scholars	Benevolences OCWM	Benevolences Other	Home Expenses	Property Values
Ala.-Miss.	11	784	372	$ 980	$ 289	$ 10,233	$ 152,400
Ga.-S.C.	13	1,340	417	773	632	10,970	250,576
Louisiana	13	1,170	439	577	741	15,983	70,700
N.C. Chr.	97	10,247	3,615	381	175	26,537	255,600
N.C. Cong'l	43	2,006	1,978	936	636	22,066	242,750
Tenn.-Ky.	8	1,135	385	986	430	9,706	269,400
Texas-Okla.	13	394	256	391	195	4,382	49,850
Va. Chr.	31	3,171	1,445	382	0	27,134	118,650
Totals	229	20,247	8,907	$5,406	$3,098	$127,011	$1,409,926
Chr. Only	128	13,418	5,060	$ 763	$ 175	$ 53,671	$ 364,250
Cong'l Only	101	6,829	3,847	$4,643	$2,923	$ 73,340	$1,045,676

had already been accumulated. Rather, it tended to confirm the information on record and to dispel any Pandora fancies or doubts.

Regarding the Black Congregational churches of the South, it may be noted that during the Barnwell years most areas of church life were on a downward spiral, reaching the lowest points in church and church school memberships, evangelism, extrasocioreligious activities, support of local church needs and of denominational missions in 1941, the last full administrative year of Superintendent Barnwell. At the time of his death, Barnwell had the largest and probably the most efficient, most effective staff of any period in the history of Black churches, plus the able assistance and cooperation of several pastors and lay leaders. His staff included a full-time office secretary; a director of religious education, with three assistant directors of religious education assigned to specific areas; and a director of rural church work in North Carolina and in Virginia. Together these seven persons attempted to cover the field and to extend the ministries of the staff to all Black Congregational Christian churches in the South. The enormity of this assignment cannot be overemphasized. The Christian churches were overorganized. Beside the Afro-Christian Convention and the Woman's Home and Foreign Missionary Convention, each of which claimed to be national in scope, there were seven Afro-Christian Conferences, including a very small one in New York (no churches were active in New Jersey or Pennsylvania). Each of these seven conferences had a women's convention and a Sunday school convention, each of which in turn had its own separate meetings annually. Also, none of the rural churches and barely more than a handful of city churches had full-time pastoral service.

A more serious problem was one of adjustment—to discover a midway position in administration that could be acceptable both to Black Christians and to Congregationalists or to recognize that a uniquely different approach, in administration and services, would be required in working with the Black Christian churches. In North Carolina, the only southern state in which there were both Black Christian churches and Black Congregational churches, directly after the 1931 merger, attempts were made to unite all Black Congregational and all Black Christian churches of North Carolina in a single state conference, with the five existing North Carolina conferences becoming associations of the conference, each with a geographical boundary that did not extend into another association boundary.

At least three joint meetings were held to work out satisfactory understandings and compromises. Very little was accomplished, however. Many *Christian* leaders felt that *all* Black Christian churches, including those of Virginia and of New York, should be in, and that the Afro-Christian Convention should continue to be the "over-all, national" body of the Black Congregational Christian churches. Many *Congregational* leaders contended that there should be a state conference that would include all, but only, Black Congregational Christian churches of North Carolina; and that in time the overall Black national body should be a union of the Afro-Christian Convention and the National Convention of Congregational Workers Among Negroes. Often the meetings were argumentative and highly volatile; there were wide differences as to nomenclature, parliamentary procedures, church and denominational polity, and in religious and worship patterns. How a conference should operate and relate to the General Council of Congregational Christian Churches or what really constituted a state conference was not the least of these differences.

I sat quietly through these meetings, too new in North Carolina to give counsel or to be heeded by either side. Little good resulted. Feelings were hurt and cleavages were established that have never been entirely removed. For many years, among the Black Christians, nearly all Black Congregationalists were suspect. Superintendent Barnwell was highly suspect because of his insistence that the administrative rules to which he was accustomed should apply to all alike. His authority was challenged, his appeal for denominational support went unheeded, and none of his program plans was accepted. This dissension continued to grow and reached its climax in 1941. In the winter of 1941 a special meeting of the officers of the Christian conferences of North Carolina and of Virginia was held at the Manly Street Christian Church of Raleigh, North Carolina. The meeting opened at 10 A.M., recessed for a short luncheon period, and finally adjourned at 5 P.M. All complaints and grievances were thoroughly aired. The 1931 merger of Congregational and Christian churches was uppermost in the thoughts of several who spoke. My notes on this meeting record the following expressions: "Most of us hardly understand what the merger is; something has clouded our vision." "The merger is not a child of our own; it was born of another group and shoved down to us. It is a fine vision, but it is not native to us or understood by us." "Has the merger proven to be satisfactory? The flat answer is 'No!' This doesn't mean that I have no faith in it; but looked at from all angles, it has not been satisfactory. We colored folk, both Congregationalists and Christians, need to come together and arrive at something or some way in which we can work together. Some of the Congregationalists have been arrogant toward us, or condescending, as if we were children. We are not children. You can lead some folk, but you can't drive them." These were some of the negative expressions.

But there were strong expressions on the other side. "Should we go farther with the merger? If we don't go any farther, what will we lose? I am sold on the idea of the merger. The merger has brought to us a fellowship that we can't afford to lose. It is the will of God that we be one in purpose and in aim. The merger gives us more culture, stronger leaders who are willing to pull 50-50 with us; it gives us full-time religious workers who visit among our churches and provide summer conferences for our young people, institutes and training for ministers and laity; annuities and old-age pensions are open to us—things we never had before." "Yes, we had Franklinton College, but it was owned by the General Christian Convention or a board of control that was appointed by the convention, and it would have been lost if the Congregationalists had not saved it for us."

At the close of the day no decision had been reached. The matter of withdrawal from the denomination was tabled; a 1942 spring meeting of ministers and laity of the several conferences was planned, at which a definite decision as to withdrawal and the reorganization of the Black Christian Church would be made. (Superintendent Barnwell died on March 1, 1942, and the spring meeting was never convened.)

I was the only Congregationalist invited to these meetings.

103

Others came but were not admitted. One other staff member, who was of Christian background, was present—Merlissie Ross Tyson (Mrs. John A. Middleton). She served as secretary of the meeting. Three prominent leaders in this meeting at Raleigh— the Rev. F.A. Hargett, of the Eastern Atlantic Conference; the Rev. Charles A. Harris, of the Eastern Virginia Conference; and the Rev. Joseph D. Farrar, president of the Afro-Christian Convention—were the same three persons who were largely responsible for my election as successor to Henry Barnwell.

Considerable space has been given to this Raleigh meeting because of its importance. It was charged with feelings of anger and of wounded pride, but there was no explosion. I have seldom seen a group more calm, more seriously deliberate in their expressions and in their determination to demand a change. In my opinion, this Raleigh meeting was the turning point in the relationship of Black Christians to the denomination and especially of Black Christians and Black Congregationalists in the South.

All attempts at uniting Black Congregational and Christian churches or conferences and associations in North Carolina had failed, but the cause was not lost.

Shortly after the merger Phoebe Fraser became director of Christian education and spent a large portion of her time working among the young people and their leaders of the Christian churches of North Carolina and of Virginia. A forceful speaker, she was sought by all the Christian conferences and conventions. In 1936 the first Young People's Summer Conference, patterned somewhat after the Kings Mountain Youth Conference, was held at Franklinton Christian College. The old college dormitory and classrooms were reopened. The furniture was overused and inadequate; the water supply was limited; the plumbing was quite uncertain; and it was easier to buy the food already prepared than to cook it on the worn-out kitchen range. But the people came, over 100 of them. Parents came with their children; many willing workers came who cleaned up fallen plaster, put up window shades, scrubbed floors, cleared the campus of debris, mowed the grass and weeds, and established play areas for the children and young people.

Despite the discomfort and serious overcrowding, this summer conference was a grand, soul-stirring experience for the Black Christians of North Carolina and of Virginia. It was their hope that the Christian college could be resurrected for the use of Black Christian churches. The new name of Franklinton Center was adopted, and each year a Young People's Summer Conference and a daily vacation Bible school were conducted at the center. Franklinton Center became the mecca for the Black Christian churches of North Carolina and of Virginia.

In the winter of 1936–37 the first institute for in-service training of ministers was held at Franklinton Center. This institute ran for four weeks and provided classes in Bible, English, preparation and delivery of sermons, planning the worship service, and such. Over forty ministers attended the institute. The Rev. Carl R. Key, pastor of the Holland (Virginia) Christian Church, was dean, or director of the institute. During this first session and for thirty years thereafter it was my privilege to teach classes in the ministers' institute at Franklinton Center. Through these years I worked with the Rev. Robert Lee House, the Rev. William M. Lake, the Rev. William R. Brogden, Dr. Ross W. Sanderson, Dr. W. Judson King, directors of the Center at Franklinton, North Carolina or at its present location near Enfield (Bricks), North Carolina. This institute made a valuable contribution, especially to pastors who were serving Black churches in North Carolina and in Virginia.

In connection with the ministers' institute a retreat for leaders in women's work was held, usually the last week of the institute, which brought together large numbers of women for training in women's work and in related church activities. Later, under the direction of Leila W. Anderson, a Christian education institute was started. This institute was well attended by Sunday school officers and teachers of the churches of North Carolina and of Virginia. To complete the regular activities of the center, there was a weekend retreat for laypersons who were active in their churches as leaders but who could be free only for weekend activities. Franklinton Center at Franklinton, North Carolina could comfortably house seventy-five or eighty people; the new center at Bricks, North Carolina had dormitory space for 120. Every year both were filled for the Young People's Summer Conference. In fact, facilities at Old Franklinton Center were never adequate for the youth conferences. From 100 to 130 people came to each conference, so that bedrooms, classrooms, and the dining room were overcrowded. Many who had not even registered came, and no one was ever turned away. Other church-related activities were well attended but, except for the Christian education institute, were never overcrowded.

Expenses for all these activities were kept at a minimum. The conference staff or the national boards provided basic leadership for all these events, supplemented by selected area ministers and lay leaders. Enough adults—often parents—came with the young people to provide desired chaperonage and considerable free services in the kitchen, in the dining room, and in other places where service was needed. Each conference in North Carolina and in Virginia set aside money for a scholarship for each minister who attended the ministers' institute. Many churches gave full scholarships to young people who attended summer conferences.

Two other Young People's Summer Conferences operated for the Black churches of the South. The oldest was the Kings Mountain (North Carolina) Summer Conference, with Superintendent Barnwell as the director. The Rev. Edward H. Phillips, founder of the Kamp Knighton (Louisiana) Conference, was its only director during his lifetime. Neither of these men, however, participated in the activities at Franklinton Center. Kamp Knighton was named for Dr. W. Knighton Bloom, extension secretary of the Congregational Sunday School Extension Society, whose warm friendship and financial encouragement made it possible for Mr. Phillips to establish Kamp Knighton on an attractive acreage on Bayou Teche, three miles from New Iberia. This center served the Morbihan community and the Black Congregational churches of Louisiana and of Texas. The Kings Mountain conference was held at Lincoln Academy, an elementary school and high school sponsored by the American Missionary Association. This conference sought to serve all Black Congregational churches of the Southeast, from North Carolina to Texas. Travel for ministers was subsidized on a graduated scale, so that a pastor from Greensboro, North Carolina who attended the conference had personal expenses about equal to those of a pastor from Houston, Texas. There were activities and classes for ministers, churchwomen, and young people; and vacation Bible school for children under twelve. Kings Mountain was the ideal after which all other Black Congregational Christian conferences and camps in the Southeast were patterned.

Kings Mountain was also the town house meeting place for Black ministers and church leaders across the South. Here they came together for eight days, with enough leisure time—after worship, study, recreation, and other conference routine—for serious discussions of the problems and the needs of their churches. These discussions were often lengthy and were critical of American Missionary Association methods of administration, of waning interest and of lack of know-how in religious work among Negroes, and of retrenchment in financial assistance to Black churches of the South. There was some hostility toward the association and toward superintendents who were appointed by the AMA without consultation with the field. American Missionary Association secretaries often met with the ministers to hear their complaints and recommendations. A Council of Seven, made up of moderators or presidents of Black conferences or conventions of the South, was formed to meet with the superintendent as an advisory board or committee. This approach was different. It provided feedback from the field and gave outstanding leaders across the field opportunity to share in the program planning and the prosecution of the work among the Black Congregational Christian churches of the South. The most important result of deliberations and recommendations of the Council of Seven was the transfer, in 1936, of southern Black church work from the American Missionary Association to the Congregational Home Missionary Society. In a report given at the annual meeting of the association, held at Mount Holyoke College, South Hadley, Massachusetts, June 1936, Superintendent Barnwell stated that

> the Strategy Committee has taken the decisive step which transferred the supervision of Southern Negro churches to the Home Missionary Society. *Aunt Mary Ann,* as the Association is fondly called, has nurtured us carefully along with her schools, which came into being at the same time; indeed, some of the churches grew out of the schools. The

question comes, "Why the transfer?" The answer, "Why not?"

There followed a defining of the interest and expertise of the American Missionary Association as being primarily educational, and that of the Congregational Home Missionary Society as being exclusively evangelical and church-extension oriented. The American Missionary Association agreed to continue its appropriation for Black church work in the South for five years, but all other responsibilities for the work were transferred to the Home Missionary Society.

Superintendent Barnwell's report continued:

During this year of uncertainty our work has not become stagnant. Perhaps the most outstanding accomplishments have been in our Department of Religious Education, newly created with the Atlanta Office and directed by Miss Phoebe L. Fraser. In our efforts to establish trends toward vital religious experience, we have, in this department, stressed particularly:

Leadership Training Institutes and Classes
How to Introduce Better Worship Services
Field Visitation, Guided by "Church Year" Programs
Workers' Conferences
Workers' and Young People's Summer Conferences
Student Summer Service Program
Christian Life Conferences (Retreats—Youth, 14-18, 18-24)

With the impetus of the Department of Religious Education, the cooperation of the entire field, and the judicious supervision of the Extension Boards, we feel sure that the new church year will not fall short . . . in proving that the Southern Negro Churches are marching forward with unswerving faith toward the fullfillment of their task.

This optimism was not borne out by statistics. Decline among the former Congregational churches of the South in all significant areas continued. Only the former Christian churches showed significant increases, due at least in part to a more complete listing of the churches and to better reporting. It is true, however, that the department of religious education was doing significant and impressive work under the leadership of Phoebe Fraser. The three conference centers—Franklinton, Kings Mountain, and Kamp Knighton—received enthusiastic support for whatever activities were planned at these centers. The student summer service program was enlarged; it provided seminarians as summer pastors for vacant churches and trained workers, who not only conducted vacation Bible schools in many churches but who worked zealously, especially with the youth and the women of these churches, in daily activities. In many instances playgrounds were started and young people and children were organized into clubs. These innovative activities stimulated many local leaders to cooperate with the student workers and to continue many of these activities after the workers were gone. The Christian life conferences were a revival of an idea that was started by the first extension worker, as early as 1924. These conferences were localized and brought together youth and their adult leaders from many geographically convenient groups of churches across the South. Whether these were called Christian life conferences, youth revivals, or youth rallies, the purpose was the same: to involve the youth in the work and life of the church and to seek their enthusiastic commitment to Christ.

The fifth-Sunday union meeting was a unique development among Black town-and-country Christian churches that had preaching services only once or twice each month. For most of these churches and for their pastors the fifth Sunday was a free Sunday, except for the union meetings. These meetings moved from church to church, brought together good representation from most of the churches, and provided a full day: Sunday school; worship service, including a sermon; plenty of wholesome food served at the church and shared by all. In the afternoon there was an excellent program of music, readings, and informative lectures. The day concluded with a business session in which reports were given, and the place of meeting and speakers for next fifth-Sunday union meeting were selected. These meetings were well attended and were well planned by officers, who were elected annually.

The new emphases on religious education and on youth work were national in scope. In *missionary conferences* the Congregational Home Missionary Society, the Sunday School Extension Society, and the Congregational Education Society gave both staff and financial assistance in these areas. With the continued budget support of the American Missionary Association and the cutting off of financial aid to most of the small town-and-country churches across the South, the *Atlanta office* (Superintendent Barnwell) was able to enlarge the staff of the department of religious education and to extend the services of this department quite generously toward the *Christian* churches of North Carolina and of Virginia. These innovative religious activities were received most enthusiastically by the Black Christians, as were the leaders in this department—Phoebe Fraser (Mrs. Burney), director; Merlissie Tyson (Mrs. Middleton) and Kate Lassiter (Mrs. Jones), assistants; and the Rev. J. Taylor Stanley, director of rural church work. At least one of the four of us attended all annual convention, conference, district, and association meetings and as many of the union meetings as possible.

With the merger of the Congregational and Christian churches, Superintendent Barnwell became overextended and overworked. Attendance at all conference and association meetings was a must, but nearly all other meetings of the area had to be touched through other staff members. Jim Crow conditions in the South made travel by train or by bus demeaning. Even when motoring, few rest rooms were open to Blacks; and decent overnight lodging or palatable meals along highways were rarely, if ever, available to Blacks. Often one had to drive many extra miles to find the welcome mat of a parish home. Yet Henry Barnwell, month after month, year after year, tried desperately to cover the South, visiting the churches, counseling with pastors and church leaders, and participating in a variety of programs and services. He also spent a goodly portion of his time in the Atlanta office working on field correspondence, writing monthly reports and requisitions to the New York office, editing a conference paper (*The Southern News, The Regional News, The Amistad*), and still tried to find a little time for family and personal needs.

Cutting off financial aid to unproductive small churches made it possible to give greater assistance to selected churches where social ministries and specialized types of religious and community activities were developed. Points that received special attention and financial support included churches in Beaumont, Texas; New Orleans, Louisiana; Winston-Salem, Raleigh, and Wilmington, North Carolina; Lexington and Louisville, Kentucky. Most of these churches provided a kindergarten or nursery, a more or less equipped playground, a community center for social services and social gatherings, scouting for boys and girls, and productive activities for the women of the church, such as sewing, cooking, and flower culture.

The Graham Church of Beaumont, Texas is an excellent example of a church that engaged in specialized ministries. The playground was equipped with swings, slides, and other apparatus and sported a beautifully kept tennis court. A cub pack and a scout troop met regularly under the direction of trained leaders. There were active clubs, other than the regular church organizations, for young people and for the women of the church and community. Surprisingly, there was a small community infirmary or hospital, with rooms for ten or twelve inpatients. It offered clinical care for expectant mothers and a delivery room. On my first visit to Beaumont, as superintendent of the Black churches, I spent a night in this hospital in a room not far removed from the delivery room. There were two deliveries that night.

The pastor and his wife, Dr. and Mrs. Charles F.L. Graham, headed and directed this program, competently assisted by a registered nurse, doctors, a dentist, a social worker, a director of recreation, kindergarten teachers, and others. Professional fees were at a minimum. For full-time workers, including the pastor and his wife, small salaries were provided through the Atlanta office. When possible, these salaries were supplemented by the church and by gifts from the Beaumont community. With the exception of the infirmary, work somewhat similar to that at Beaumont was operated at each point named above, and in lesser degree at many Black Congregational churches in the South. Elements of this type of program were the criteria that largely determined if financial assistance would be continued.

After the 1931 merger of the Congregational and Christian churches, the new denomination, to avoid duplication and waste, faced the task of redefining the mission and workings of all boards and agencies of the two uniting denominations and of harmonizing and combining these into inclusive boards and agencies of the Congregational Christian Churches. The National Council and the General Convention became the General Council of the Congregational Christian Churches. All foreign missionary work was combined under the American Board of Commissioners for Foreign Missions. By 1936 the Board of Home Missions of the Congregational Christian Churches had been formed, its divisions established, and the work of each delineated. Although many of the corporations thus brought together remained in force, all worked together under a single board of directors. State conferences were reorganized to include both Congregational and Christian ministers and churches within the geographical boundaries of the conference. In the North, Black ministers and churches were included, although there was still a director of Negro church work in the North—a position Harold M. Kingsley had held for many years.

While Negro work was included in the Southeast District, it remained a racially segregated and separate missionary unit of the Southeast and of the denomination.

Dr. Edwin C. Gillette, whose headquarters were in Jacksonville, Florida, was superintendent of the Southeast District; the Rev. Henry S. Barnwell was associate superintendent, in charge of Negro churches in the South. Beginning in 1921, Barnwell had to struggle through many momentous changes in Negro church work in the South and in his own relationships and responsibilities to it. World War I, the Great Migrations, the Daniel Report and the resultant recommendations, the merger and the attending reorganization of the new denomination, the transfer of his work to a new and financially weaker division of the Board of Home Missions, and the expansion of his territory to include another state and 138 more churches all helped to aggravate his problems. Superintendent Barnwell was the person most aware of, most concerned with, and most affected by these changes. These concerns were shared with Black church leaders in special meetings during the fall and winter of 1941–42. Meetings were held in New Orleans, in Birmingham, and in Atlanta; the final meeting was held at the Wentz Memorial

Church, Winston-Salem, North Carolina. Church leaders of North Carolina and of Virginia had been invited. The leaders of Christian conferences were conspicuously absent. Here Henry Barnwell not only shared his concerns with the Black leaders but interpreted with enthusiasm the new directions for church work under the church extension division of the Board of Home Missions.

At the close of the Winston-Salem meeting I returned to my parish in Dudley, North Carolina. Superintendent Barnwell drove to Mebane for the night. The next day, Saturday, while en route to the Lassiter home in Strieby, North Carolina, where he was to spend the night, he visited with friends in Melville, Greensboro, and Asheboro. Sunday, March 1, 1942, he was out early to keep a preaching engagement with Pastor George Hannar and the St. Luke Church of Goldston, North Carolina and was expected to return to speak at the evening service. He never returned. In his eagerness to contact as many ministers and churches as possible, he spent the afternoon visiting in Sanford, Moncure, and Broadway. He died of a heart attack on the road back to St. Luke Church.

Superintendent Henry S. Barnwell used his life in the work that he loved, often driving himself beyond reasonable endurance, under the most trying circumstances in his beloved Southland; he gave all his best years in service to his people and to the Black Congregational churches in the South.

After his death, members of his staff continued to carry out the work plans that had been made, including attendance of a denominational meeting in Philadelphia; also, at least one staff member attended the spring meetings of the state conferences (associations) southeast of North Carolina and of Virginia. With considerable co-opted help, youth conferences and camps went on almost as usual. Phoebe Fraser Burney gave excellent leadership and direction at Kings Mountain and at Franklinton Center. Edward H. Phillips carried on in his inimitable way at Kamp Knighton in Louisiana. Outside help included the Rev. and Mrs. Charles F. Rush at Kings Mountain; Susie I. Gregory, Lucille Jones, and the Rev. J.D. Farrar at Franklinton Center; and the Rev. Henderson H. Dunn, the Rev. John T. Enwright, the Rev. John D. Moore, and Dr. Norman A. Holmes at Kamp Knighton. Student summer service was continued, and eight students were commissioned, at the Kings Mountain Summer Conference, for work during the summer of 1942. Merlissie R. Tyson (Middleton) and I continued our duties in North Carolina and in Virginia, working full time at the Kings Mountain and the Franklinton conferences, serving extensively at Sunday school conventions, youth gatherings, and attending a few fifth-Sunday union meetings, as well as monitoring student summer service work in our area.

At the Atlanta office the Rev. Caesar S. Ledbetter, pastor of Plymouth Congregational Church in Charleston, South Carolina and a member of the board of directors of the Board of Home Missions, was asked to give supervision, but the main work of the office was done by Phoebe Fraser Burney, until a successor to Superintendent Barnwell was elected and took charge of the work, on October 1, 1942.

Chapter 8

The J. Taylor Stanley Years

One of the great surprises of my life came in June 1942, when I was chosen to succeed Henry S. Barnwell as associate superintendent of Black Congregational Christian churches of the South. Earlier in June, at the Kings Mountain Summer Conference, Congregational ministers met to nominate a successor to Barnwell. Because I was not informed of the meeting, I was off campus and missed most of it. When I returned, the voting was over. The Rev. Charles F. Rush, pastor of Emmanuel Church, Charlotte, North Carolina, was the unanimous choice. Dr. William J. Faulkner, Dr. Henry Curtis McDowell, and Dr. Norman A. Holmes were appointed to convey this action to executives of the extension division of the Board of Home Missions meeting at the 1942 session of the General Council in Durham, New Hampshire. All ministers at the Kings Mountain meeting had agreed that none of them would accept a nomination.

In Durham there was insistence that the Black Christian churches should have equal representation with the Black Congregational churches. As a result, nine persons were brought together as an election committee: Dr. Ernest M. Haliday and Dr. Thomas A. Tripp of the extension division; Dr. William T. Scott, general superintendent of the Southeast District; Dr. William J. Faulkner, Dr. Norman A. Holmes, and Dr. Henry Curtis McDowell of the Black Congregational churches; and the Rev. Joseph D. Farrar, the Rev. Frederick A. Hargett, and the Rev. Charles A. Harris of the Black Christian churches. Both Charles Rush and I were nominated. The Kings Mountain men felt inspired and were determined that Rush should be elected. The other six were just as determined in my regard but worked for unanimity, hoping that the new superintendent would not begin with a conference divided along old denominational lines.

For two evenings Dr. Faulkner met with me to persuade me to accept the nomination. My response was negative. At the close of our second session Dr. Faulkner asked if I would meet with him, Dr. Haliday, Dr. Tripp, and Dr. Scott. I consented to the meeting. The final outcome was that I was elected associate superintendent, in charge of Negro church work in the South. I agreed to sever pastoral relations with the First Congregational Christian Church of Dudley, North Carolina and to begin work as superintendent by October 1, 1942. William J. Faulkner was largely responsible for my acceptance of the work. But even more, I was indebted to the three Black Christian ministers who would have no other and who stood by until they were assured of my election. This was a debt I could not ignore. My responsibility was to *all* Black Congregational and Christian churches in the South.

There were many problems that had to be dealt with immediately, many adjustments to be made. The Atlanta office was reasonably central to Black Congregational churches in the South. The merger had moved the center of the Black church population to some point in North Carolina. I chose Greensboro. The budget for Negro church work in the South was painfully limited and was carefully watched and restricted, wherever possible, by the New York office. By the end of my first year as superintendent the staff for Negro church work in the South had been reduced to two persons—a superintendent and an office secretary-director of Christian education, with annual salaries of $2,750 and $1,500, respectively; travel allowances for each; no house or residence allowance; and no expense allowance while at the home base. To live honestly was a real problem. Many churches and conferences were willing to share and did, in fact, give many items of food, for example, as well as cash gifts, but we were *required* to report *all* money received from the field as missionary contributions.

Many times travel was a serious problem. In North Carolina and in Virginia most of the churches were country churches, often located on or near unimproved roads, and could only be reached by car. Trains and buses in the South were strictly segregated; many bus drivers, train conductors, and even Black porters were frequently disagreeable, defiant, and unconcerned about the comfort or welfare of Black passengers. Along the highways very few comfort or eating facilities were open to Blacks. Even in the larger cities one could rarely find decent meals or overnight lodging. Our limited expense allowance made travel by plane or Pullman prohibitive.

Two problems that were more difficult to handle were the wide differences in cultural and religious patterns and the lack of communication between Christians and Congregationalists, even in North Carolina. For these and other reasons, hostilities on all sides had to be understood and dealt with. For several years Black Congregationalists in the South had been clamoring for a voice in the administration and in the direction of their own church work, as evidenced by the appointment of the Council of Seven, who served as an advisory board to Superintendent Barnwell; and as further evidenced by the appointment, at Kings Mountain, of a committee, representative of the Black Congregational churches, to nominate and to share in the election of their superintendent. They did not anticipate that this would be shared equally by the Black Christians. I was the first superintendent of Negro work in the South in whose election representatives of the Black churches had shared.

Other adjustments and decisions were made: to move the office from Atlanta, via Dudley, North Carolina, to Greensboro; to move my family from a delightful rural parish, where all of us had warm friendships, to the city; to adjust my schedule so that my ministry could be shared equitably with all the churches; to refuse to establish residence at Franklinton Center, Franklinton, North Carolina and to take on the added responsibilities of directing center activities. By the summer of 1943, however, we were able to settle in Greensboro, North Carolina.

My first visits to the Atlanta office were exploratory. The Rev. Caesar S. Ledbetter and Phoebe Fraser Burney were in charge of the office. They gave much needed cooperation and guidance as to the office setup. A casual study of the files of correspondence, reports, and financial records revealed certain disturbing facts.

1. The merger of Congregational and Christian churches had more than doubled the number of churches, tripled the number of members, as well as enlarged the geographical area of administration of Black churches in the South.

2. The decline in the number of churches, in membership,

in Sunday schools and small-group enrollment, and in missionary giving of Black Congregational churches was continuing.

3. There had been very little meaningful or effective communication between the superintendent's office and the Black Christian conferences and churches; there had been almost no communication between the Black Congregational and the Black Christian conferences and other organizations.

There were more delicate revelations, but in all, I had enough information to give direction to a course of action.

In 1943 I attended all the Congregational and Christian conferences in the South. These conferences usually ran from Wednesday or Thursday evening through Sunday afternoon. I often shared generously in the transactions of these conferences, especially in the matters of licensure and of ordination of ministers. I delivered at least one address at each and was frequently asked to preach a sermon. (Most conferences had a noonday sermon and an evening sermon each day.) All the North Carolina and the Virginia conferences met in the fall. All others met in the spring or the summer. At each I could meet nearly all the ministers and delegates from most of the churches, schedule meetings in many of the churches, and make plans for upcoming conference or regional activities. Already I had followed this pattern for four years as director of rural church work in North Carolina and in Virginia. In 1943 I visited almost every church in the other states. There were sixty-three churches listed in these states, seventeen of which were inactive or nearly so; only thirteen of the remaining forty-six had memberships that exceeded 100.

Several conference moderators and pastors were quite helpful in providing comfortable lodging and transportation to strange and out-of-the-way places. The Rev. Arthur C. Curtright, of Savannah, Georgia, transported me to every active church in Georgia and in South Carolina, as well as to communities where churches were no longer active. The Rev. Henderson H. Dunn, of New Orleans, Louisiana, and the Rev. John D. Moore, of Houston, Texas, did the same for me in their respective conferences. I came to the end of 1943 depressed and disillusioned. Except for Trinity Church in Athens, Alabama and First Church of Dudley, North Carolina, there were no church buildings under ten years old. The elegance and beauty of many of the buildings had faded; a number were badly in need of repair or replacement, and a few seemed totally abandoned.

Pastors, too, were discouraged and unenthusiastic about the future of their churches. Many of them and their wives had turned to teaching or to other employment for adequate income. What was true of these sixty-three churches in the Deep South was equally true of the forty-three Congregational churches in North Carolina. Twenty-seven of these forty-three churches had less than fifty members each. Twelve others had less than 100; four had more than 100, and the total membership of the four was only 498. Not only had I taken on administrative responsibility for 106 Black Congregational churches, as listed in the Congregational Christian *Year Book* of 1941, with a total of 6,975 members, scattered in eleven southern states, but also similar and equal responsibility for 129 Christian churches, concentrated almost entirely in North Carolina and in Virginia, with a total of 12,640 members.

Comparisons between Black Christian and Black Congregational churches in the South were inevitable. The average membership of a Congregational church was sixty-six; average membership of a Christian church was ninety-nine. Nearly all Congregational pastors had had at least some college and seminary training; many had both college and seminary degrees. Very few Christian pastors had training above the high school level; none had completed requirements for a seminary degree. The Congregationalists had had large financial assistance toward ministers' salaries and church buildings and facilities, as well as opportunity for liberal educational and religious training in church-related schools and colleges, conveniently located throughout the South. The Black Christians paid the meager ministers' salaries themselves, built their own churches, and developed their own church organizations, with very little encouragement, financial or otherwise, from their white Christian neighbors. There was only one church-related school for Black Christians to attend—Franklinton Christian College—which was never well funded and never developed, academically, beyond a good high school. These comparisons, in the minds of national and regional church leaders, gave the Black Christians a decided plus. But these are surface facts; they do not explore the essential meaning and mission of the church of Jesus Christ.

The statistics give a grim and uncertain overview of the Black churches in the South during that time. Earlier reference was made to the Daniel survey of aided Black Congregational churches in the South, conducted by William A. Daniel in 1926–27. There were sixty-three churches that received financial aid from the American Missionary Association, mostly toward pastors' salaries. The average membership of these churches was fifty-eight. The average amount paid to the pastors by the American Missionary Association was $26.87 monthly, which represented from one fourth to one half the pastor's salary. Dr. Daniel's description of church buildings and equipment showed that almost all were in great need of repair or replacement and of use and proper care. The financial aid that was being given was *too much* for the quality and competence of the leaders that were provided and *too little* to attract the pastoral leadership required to attract new members and to develop these churches into active, full-time, self-supporting churches.

By 1942–43 the picture had not improved. Twenty-three of these sixty-three churches had been abandoned, and no services of any kind were held in them. In several locations—Paris, Texas; Thibodaux, Louisiana; Mobile, Alabama; Knoxville, Tennessee; Boley, Oklahoma; Athens, Georgia; Caledonia, Mississippi—no former member could be found. Seven North Carolina Congregational churches had already been dropped or were inactive. The aided churches in North Carolina had been reduced from twenty-four to nine. However, the amount of financial aid had not been reduced substantially but had been concentrated in strategic areas that had good, youthful, pastoral leadership and had showed promise of becoming self-supporting, especially in a few churches that majored in programs of social work and community service. Outstanding among these were Graham Church, Beaumont, Texas; Wentz Memorial, Winston-Salem, North Carolina; Chandler, Lexington, Kentucky; First, Raleigh, North Carolina; Gregory, Wilmington, North Carolina; and Rush Memorial, Atlanta, Georgia. Rather rigid application of the Daniel recommendations had made these concentrations possible. But there were negative results that were still apparent at the time of Superintendent Barnwell's death.

At Dudley, in my own home and at my personal expense, I provided office space, room, and meals for the office worker. When my residence and office moved to Greensboro, the whole responsibility of renting or buying a house and of finding office space that could be rented within the limit of $12.50 per month was left to me. At $12.50 per month, the First Congregational Christian Church of Greensboro arranged for me to set up office in a section of their basement, eight rugged blocks from my residence. I had to provide my own fuel and janitorial service. The basement was always damp and was completely covered with water whenever there was considerable rain, so that cabinets, furniture, and files containing books and records had to be raised on blocks to avoid water damage.

My wife and our children were wonderful about helping to make the adjustment to our new environment and to my new life-style as a part-time husband and father; they also gave their free time to see that the office was kept comfortable, open, and in operation, whether the part-time office secretary was present or not. Their loyalty and their enthusiasm for *our* part in the life and total development of the Black churches in the South gave me new incentive and determination to change trends and to improve the quality of church leaders.

My work as pastor of the church at Dudley had brought to the parish such notable persons of the denomination as Dr. Ernest M. Haliday, Dr. James F. English, Dr. William F. Frazier, Dr. Edwin C. Gillette, Priscilla Chase, and Dr. John R. Scottford. Some of these and others had worked with me at Franklinton Center during my years as director of rural church work in North Carolina and in Virginia; in most instances, these persons made their first contacts with the Black Christians of North Carolina and of Virginia. They were impressed that these Black Christians, with very little help beyond their own limited resources, had developed their own churches and conferences and the Afro-Christian National Convention and had operated their own school for the training of ministers and lay leaders.

The Black Christians were seen as a new opportunity for church extension and missionary action among Blacks in the South for our denomination.

Special interracial meetings, at which the Black Christian churches of North Carolina and of Virginia were a special consideration, were held in Burlington, Franklinton, and Raleigh, North Carolina and in Norfolk, Virginia. These gatherings gave all of us, the executives of denominational boards and agencies included, a chance to get acquainted with one another across racial and former church boundaries. An important outcome of such meetings was that special consideration would be given to leadership training for Black churches in North Carolina and in Virginia; this meant enriching and funding in-service training for ministers, Christian education institutes, instructive retreats for lay people, student summer service training, and camps and conferences for the youth, using Franklinton Center as a base for these extra activities to improve pastoral and lay leadership.

Immediately, certain desperate needs of Black church work in the South became apparent. The need to upgrade the quality and to lower the age level of pastoral and lay leadership in the churches was uppermost. In-service training of ministers in winter institutes of two or of even four weeks' duration was woefully limited and inadequate, but the effects were measurable in a better preaching ministry, in the improvement of worship services, and in the establishment of Franklinton Center as a mecca for the churches of North Carolina and of Virginia. All conferences of the two states and their auxiliaries were enthusiastic for the restoration of the buildings and grounds of Franklinton Center. Each made an annual contribution for this purpose. Thus, the center was restored to uncertain comfort and use.

Here the winter institute for ministers was begun. The Rev. Carl R. Key, the first director of the institute, served three years and was succeeded by the Rev. Robert Lee House. Both were white ministers of the Southern Convention. The institute was well attended by pastors, averaging over thirty-five each winter, and continued in operation until the center was moved to Bricks, North Carolina. Each conference provided scholarships to cover expenses of its own ministers who attended the institute.

The Christian education institute was developed as a three-year training experience for Sunday school officers and teachers and for adult leaders of youth work. Leila W. Anderson, who organized and directed the work, was the guiding light. Her down-to-earth approach to Bible and religious training through the church school was enthusiastically received and was attended to capacity both at Old Franklinton and at Franklinton Center at Bricks. The plan provided for first-, second-, and third-year classes, with intensive study and practice teaching for one full week each year. One who followed through for three years of satisfactory work received a certificate of merit. More importantly, these "graduates" were inspired to become more proficient leaders and teachers in the local church schools.

The Rev. Joseph H. Copeland, pastor of Zion Bethel Church of Portsmouth, Virginia, brought all his church school officers and teachers to this institute. No church in Virginia had a better organized, better attended, and more progressive Sunday school than Zion Bethel Church. As a unique "circuit rider," Leila Anderson extended her ministry in Christian education to many areas in North Carolina and in Virginia, as well as to areas in the Deep South.

This need for leadership was further met through personal contact or correspondence with a number of theological seminaries, which offered field experiences, student pastoral service, or pastoral work to Black seminarians who were approaching graduation. Student summer service became a special vehicle to these ends. Through student summer service and other types of recruiting, many present leaders of the church had their first real experience in church work and in pastoral ministry. Among these are Milton L. Upton, Oliver W. Holmes, Joseph E. Boone, Percel O. Alston, Harold D. Long, Reuben A. Shears II, UN Ambassador Andrew J. Young, Andrew L. Cooper, George Gay Jr., Yvonne Delk, Yvonne Beasley, and A. Knighton Stanley.

There was a great need for stewardship training in all the churches. Most of the people were poor and had not recovered from the Great Depression, especially those in large rural communities. They were also poor church members, however, and had little concern for the financial needs of the church. Pastors were poorly paid, most buildings were old and in poor condition, and very little was done to enhance the worship, the teaching program, or other activities, if any, or to make the church comfortable and inviting. This was true of most churches across the entire Southland. The Congregational churches were further depressed because of the delinquent loans from the church building department of the Board of Home Missions. Some churches had already abandoned buildings on which such loans had been made. Others showed no inclination to pay their loans or keep the buildings in good repair.

Another way to describe the situation of the Black churches would be to state that in 1943, out of 140 churches in North Carolina, sixty-eight were vacant (churches without pastors), fifty were yoked in multiple pastorates, leaving only twenty-two that could be regarded as full-time pastoral units. In Virginia twelve churches were vacant, eleven yoked, and eight were considered pastoral units. In all other states in the South, nineteen churches were vacant or inactive, twelve were in yoked situations, and only twenty-seven could be considered pastoral units. At best, a yoked church had regular preaching services twice each month. Many had only one pastoral visit per month, except for funerals (which were often delayed until Sunday) and special occasions, such as the annual revival. Many yoked churches had both morning and evening services on regular "preaching" Sundays. In most, Sunday school was conducted each Sunday. But on "off" Sundays the people usually attended churches of other denominations in the community, so that Sunday school was poorly attended on "off Sundays."

Most yoked churches were located in small towns or in rural communities; a few were yoked with city churches. They were usually operated and controlled by the officers of the church or by two or three of its influential members, the pastor often exercising little more than remote control. Pastors were nonresident, some living 100 miles or more from the churches they served. Salaries were small. (One pastor who served four churches received $25 per month from each, or $1,200 per year. The combined membership of these churches was 1,076.) However, most ministers were not dependent upon church "salaries"; a number of them owned their own homes. Some were successful farmers, while others taught in public schools, operated their own businesses, or found other employment that assured a decent income and comfortable living. Some city pastors, also of necessity, had other occupations, and frequently ministers' wives worked to supplement the family income.

The facts about these churches and their ministers led to certain inevitable conclusions. These churches and their conferences were *free* and *independent* institutions, not to be controlled by or amenable to any rules or regulations except their own. Even the Congregational churches were being forced painfully and with considerable bitterness to this conclusion. Likewise, the ministers were *free* and *independent.* They were "kings in their own dominions." Through personal sacrifices they had "vested interests" in their churches. They were justly proud of their accomplishments and deserved respect and acceptance as ministers of the gospel.

There were strong indications that the superintendent of Black churches in the South had indeed very little executive authority over *free* and *independent* churches and ministers. No commands could be given and no demands had to be respected. The superintendent's chief function was to be minister to the ministers; a roving, compassionate, understanding friend and missionary to the people of *all* denominational Black churches. But this new definition of the duties of a superintendent had to be made convincingly clear to the ministers and to the churches: that the superintendent was their friend, one not over them but with them, who had a genuine concern for the well-being of the ministers and the churches. To create this relationship between superintendent and the Black churches of the South was no easy task, but it was essential to any progressive development of church work in the South.

During the first years most of my invitations were my own. I prepared my own schedules, usually covering periods of ten days to two weeks. With road maps or train schedules before me I planned trips to include one church each night, except Saturday, and two or three churches each Sunday. I included all churches along the route and sent a copy of the schedule to the pastor or to the church clerk if the church were vacant or if the pastor was nonresident. When possible, my first visit was with the pastor, who often accompanied me to the church, introduced me to the church officers, and arranged for my overnight care in someone's home. The meetings planned were seldom mass meetings but brought together serious and influential leaders of the church, giving everyone an opportunity to get acquainted with one another and to explore mutual interests and concerns. If no meeting had been set up, I spent the time visiting people in their homes, so that the same purpose was served. Nearly every Sunday I preached at the morning and the evening services and frequently spoke at an afternoon service at one to three churches per Sunday. Upon invitation, I also preached weeknights and at many sessions of conventions, conferences, and associations. While I welcomed an opportunity to present the denominational programs and needs, I religiously avoided "shop talk" in the worship services.

Essentially, this pattern was followed during the first five years of my superintendency. I had made lasting friendships (and perhaps a few enemies) across the South. I had established confidence in the office of the superintendent and in my own sincerity and integrity as a Christian minister, as well as in my sensitivity to the aspirations and needs of the churches. In conferences and conventions I emphasized regularly the polity and program of the denomination; the need for better salaries for pastors and for more service from them; the need for better organization and program, especially for youth, in our churches; the need for larger giving to support missions as well as the local church; and of course, the need for better buildings and facilities for worship, church school, and other activities.

Gradually, through the early years, the groundwork was laid for an organization that would include all Black Congregational Christian churches of the South on a mutual and representative basis—the Convention of the South. There were delicate emotional attachments to be dealt with. The Afro-Christian Convention had continued its biennial meetings but was in serious decline. Its auxiliary, the Woman's National Home and Foreign Missionary Convention, was perhaps stronger and accounted for a large portion of the attendance at Afro-Christian Convention meetings. There were strong ties to both organizations and to their leaders. Joseph D. Farrar, Charles A. Harris,

Junius O. Lee, Raleigh R. Briggs, and Robert J. Alston, of Virginia; and James A. Henderson, Frederick A. Hargett, J.M. Burwell Sr., J.P. Mangrum, J.W. Meadows, J.D. Hill, P.R. DeBerry, Richard D. Bullock Sr., S.W. Albright, and N.E. Higgs, of North Carolina were all active in the Afro-Christian Convention. Prominent leaders of the Woman's Home and Foreign Missionary Convention included Pearlie M. Lee, Mae W. Stephens, Ella Terry, Sarah Epps, Eliza Alexander, Bertha Goodson, Ella Cheatham, Arnetta Brown, Aurora Lee Taylor, Annie M. Moseley, Polly Simmons, and Maggie Milteer, of North Carolina; and Susie I. Gregory, Stella Parker, Mary Lou Holland, Molly Brown, Ruth Lawrence, Ada Chapman, Cora Washington, and Ruth Fulcher, of Virginia. Together, these were among the most loyal, active, and respected leaders in the local churches and conferences and in other local organizations. Some were well trained; all made up for any lack of training by their devotion to the Afro-Christian denomination.

Among Black Congregationalists there was a similar, if weaker, emotional attachment to the National Association of Congregational Workers Among Negroes. This association, in its best years—the 1920's—had held its biennial meetings at such points as Atlanta, Georgia; Washington, D.C.; Chattanooga, Tennessee; and Detroit, Michigan. It had attracted attendance from all Black Congregational churches, north and south, and from "workers among Negroes," especially of the American Missionary Association and its Black colleges. Many "workers" were white. This organization also had declined. During the early years of my superintendency this association was little more than a rump group that held caucus meetings at General Council sessions to work out stratagems to strengthen the position of the Black churches and of their leaders in the Congregational Christian denomination. Just as the Afro-Christian organizations were made up entirely of Afro-Christian churches and were controlled and directed by their leaders, so the national association was made up largely of Black Congregationalists who were in control of the organization. There was one important difference: Except for five churches with a combined membership of less than 300, all Afro-Christians were in the South, concentrated in North Carolina and in Virginia;

Black Congregationalists were scattered over eleven southern states, seven northern states, and the District of Columbia. The largest concentration of churches was in North Carolina. These simple facts of geography emphasized the urgent need for an organization that would include all Black Congregational Christian churches in the South.

Chapter 9

The Birth of the Convention
of the South

Prior to the merger of Congregational and Christian churches, in 1931, and even until the 1936 transfer of Negro church work in the South from the American Missionary Association division to the church extension division of the Board of Home Missions, the Black Congregational churches of the South were frequently designated as American Missionary Association churches. Under the church extension division all Black Congregational Christian churches in the South became part of the Southeast District, with a general superintendent of the Southeast and associate superintendents of Florida and Georgia; of Kentucky, Tennessee, and Alabama; and of Negro churches in the South. A South Central District included white Congregational Christian churches of Arkansas, Louisiana, Oklahoma, and Texas. Both the Southeast and the South Central were missionary districts; that is, they were dependent upon the Board of Home Missions for the financing of administrative and field services, for the budget for special projects, and for salaries for pastors and paid workers in promising situations. The Southern Convention, an independent conference of white churches, included all of North Carolina and of Virginia. (In 1937 the Southern Conference included Capron Bridge, Timber Mountain, West Virginia; High View, Timber Ridge, West Virginia; and Circular Church, Charleston, South Carolina in its schedule. Timber Mountain was dropped in 1938. The High View Church continued in the Southern Conference until new conference boundaries of the United Church of Christ were established. It is now in the Central Atlantic Conference.) The Negro church work of the South was more or less scattered in all southern states except Florida—the area generally covered by the South Central and the Southeast districts and the Southern Convention. There had been no serious attempt to organize all

Black churches of the South into a single, workable conference unit.

Certain oblique and overt actions of church extension division executives and of the southern white churches themselves were aimed at encouraging the southern churches, Black and white, to organize into sensible conference units. Florida was first to move from under the umbrella of the Southeast District and rapidly became a vigorous independent conference. The Central South Conference followed in 1947 and the Southeast Convention in 1949. The Southeast District had disintegrated, leaving the Black churches of the South to struggle independently with their unique and baffling problems of organization and of ways and means of financial support. In this struggle the Board of Home Missions gave full cooperation and counsel.

In the winter of 1948 a special meeting was held at First Church, Atlanta, Georgia. An executive and/or a representative of each Black conference or convention of the South was invited to attend this meeting, all expenses paid. Dr. Stanley U. North, the Rev. Ira D. Black, and the Rev. Thomas A. Tripp attended. We all worked for two days and nights to develop a plan for organization and a proposed constitution for the Convention of the South. A ten-year schedule for becoming an independent conference was proposed and tentatively adopted by the group. The superintendent was invited to attend the meeting of the board of directors of the Board of Home Missions, the summer of 1949, at Colorado Springs, Colorado, and to present the recommendations of our Atlanta group for board approval.

The initial meeting of the Convention of the South was held June 1950 at St. Stephens Congregational Christian Church, Greensboro, North Carolina. Here, the Convention of the South originated. The Rev. Frederick A. Hargett, pastor of the entertaining church, was elected president of the convention. The Rev. Joseph D. Farrar, a former president of the Afro-Christian Convention, was elected treasurer, a position he held until the Convention of the South merged with the Southern Convention and the Southern Synod, to form the Southern Conference of the United Church of Christ.

At the Greensboro meeting the recommendations of the Atlanta group were adopted. The proposed constitution was presented and finally approved for adoption at the next meeting of the convention. Important provisions of the Constitution were:

1. that each minister who had standing in a member conference or association of the convention was a voting member of the convention; that each member church shall have one voting delegate (plus one for each 300 members or major fraction thereof above the first 300).

2. that there should be a woman's fellowship, a layman's fellowship, and a youth fellowship, operating as departments of the convention under their own elected leaders.

3. that there should be a board of trustees whose voting members would be the president, secretary, and treasurer of the convention (3); the president of each fellowship (3); the elected head or an elected representative of each conference (12).

There were other provisions—delineation of duties of the superintendent, officers, and trustees; schedules of meetings; and the like.

By the close of this meeting the Convention of the South and its board of trustees became a reality, the three departments were established, and a plan for becoming a self-supporting, independent conference was adopted. The plan provided that the initial appropriation from the Board of Home Missions to the budget of the Convention of the South should be reduced by 10 percent a year over a ten-year period; and that the Convention of the South should retain 75 percent of apportionment (Our Christian World Mission) receipts and must increase its missionary giving at least enough to sustain its budget and to provide for any expansion of program or rise in cost of operation. The Convention of the South and its board of trustees should elect its own superintendent and other employed staff, plan its own budget, envision and execute its own stratagems and policies. This was a great step forward for the Black Congregational Christian churches of the South.

The following statistics show in part what was happening, in certain areas, to the life and the development of Black churches and of the Convention of the South.

The above charts do not indicate the number of ministers who had standing in the Convention of the South. However, in

The Convention of the South—Congregational Christian Churches

1951

Conferences	No. Chs.	Membership	S.S. Scholars	OCWM Gifts	Other Gifts	Home Expenses	Property Value
Ala.-Miss.	10	678	176	$1,481	$2,248	$ 8,130	$ 120,800
Ga.-S.C.	10	1,145	420	1,643	1,688	30,542	453,000
N.C.	141	12,926	5,111	2,302	3,236	69,981	1,036,150
Plymouth	20	1,271	663	732	232	42,542	250,458
Tenn.-Ky.	8	954	362	1,900	2,935	31,894	411,000
Virginia	32	4,208	1,752	563	1,648	28,212	313,650
Totals	221	21,182	8,484	$8,621	$11,987	$211,301	$2,585,058

1961

Conferences	No. Chs.	Membership	S.S. Scholars	OCWM Gifts	Other Gifts	Home Expenses	Property Value
Ala.-Miss.	11	816	356	$2,758	$3,686	$ 21,299	$ 224,000
Ga.-S.C.	10	1,345	608	4,437	6,197	47,808	673,000
N.C.	125	13,388	6,149	7,038	13,743	140,908	2,105,000
Plymouth	15	1,557	499	6,793	7,716	80,597	489,000
Tenn.-Ky.	8	960	420	3,104	4,466	49,432	292,000
Virginia	31	4,384	2,181	4,699	7,793	53,753	488,000
Totals	200	22,450	10,213	$28,829	$43,601	$393,797	$4,271,000

1951 there were 144 Black ministers and in 1961, 173 ministers.

Although the number of churches in the Convention of the South continued to decline, measurable progress was being made in all other areas. Church membership and church school enrollment were moving up gradually. The progress in financial support of national and local benevolences and of the budget of the local church was most gratifying. There were comparable advances in the salaries of pastors and in other paid services. The value of church property nearly doubled in this ten-year period, due largely to the purchase of better church buildings and equipment; the building of new, more attractive and serviceable buildings; or the extensive remodeling and furnishing of existing buildings. One or more of these procedures took place in each conference in the Convention of the South. Almost every new building was of masonry construction and provided, in addition to a sanctuary, complete facilities for educational and community service programs. The division of church extension and evangelism and its church building department gave continuous cooperation. Dr. Stanley U. North, Dr. Wesley A. Hotchkiss, the Rev. Ira D. Black, and William Kincaid Newman were regular visitors in the churches and in the conferences of the convention. They gave wise counsel in problem areas and generous help toward program plans, leadership recruitment, and building projects. It was a reasonable assumption that the Convention of the South was moving effectively toward becoming a self-supporting, self-directing conference of the Congregational Christian Churches.

The spiritual forces that were at work cannot be measured or evaluated by statistics; these forces removed many of the suspicions, healed the hostilities, and made it possible to work together in the convention and in its fellowships. Meetings of the Afro-Christian Convention were held only in North Carolina and in Virginia. Meetings of the Convention of the South were held in Greensboro (twice) and in Raleigh, North Carolina; also in Savannah and in Atlanta (twice), Georgia and in Talladega, Alabama. This tended to equalize the transportation costs for each area. Election of officers for the convention and for its departments was by popular vote, and the offices were rather evenly distributed between the Christians and the Congregationalists.

The strongest of the fellowships was the Woman's Fellowship. The former Woman's Home and Foreign Missionary Convention brought to the Woman's Fellowship most of its enrollment, as well as most of the structures of the old convention. At first the officers of the former missionary convention were reluctant to share offices that they had held, but by 1961 both *Congregational* and *Christian* women had, at some time, held every office in the Woman's Fellowship. The women learned to work together and gave generous support to projects of the Convention of the South and of the denomination.

The Layman's Fellowship and the Youth Fellowship were organized initially at the meeting of the Convention of the South and had none of the transitional problems of the Woman's Fellowship. Both organizations added popular strength to the convention and held informative, inspiring meetings. The director of christian education of the Convention of the South worked with Youth Fellowship officers in planning the programs and in carrying the enthusiasm of these meetings into the local churches.

The board of trustees of the Convention of the South met semiannually, usually in Greensboro, North Carolina, at the home of the superintendent. The executive committee of this board met quarterly; two of its meetings were held concurrently with board meetings. The president of the convention presided at all board meetings. This board became the policy-making body of the Convention of the South and increasingly accepted responsibility "to envision programs and stratagems for the growth and development of the work, and the promotion of the same . . . and to perform for the Convention all other functions, administrative and legal, which are peculiar to such Boards."

Camps and conference centers were a sort of specialty development of the Black churches of the South. The oldest and most highly developed of these was the Kings Mountain Summer Conference. Its scenic setting was ideal. Attendance was usually so high that it crowded the facilities of Lincoln Academy. First organized in 1924, it reached its zenith in the 1940s and served for a number of years as a retreat for all age groups and as a training ground for student pastors and student summer service workers. This conference center ceased operation

134

with the closing of Lincoln Academy and the sale of its property.

"Kamp Knighton, the Beautiful" was located on Bayou Teche, near New Iberia, Louisiana. The camp was organized in 1925 by Edward H. Phillips, a Spanish-American War veteran. He directed activities at the camp until his death, in 1949. Phillips' Creole heritage and his war experiences gave a unique color to the Kamp Knighton Center that made it different from all others. The barracks that housed the men and boys was a replica of old army barracks. The girls and women were much better housed, on the second floor of Eliza Phillips Hall, which was erected as a memorial to Phillips' wife. It was the only substantial building on the grounds. The ground floor provided a kitchen and a pantry, a small office and living quarters for the director, and a large all-purpose room—dining room-classroom-assembly room and playroom in the evenings and whenever the rain or heat discouraged outdoor activity.

The Kamp Knighton property was owned by the Louisiana Congregational Christian Conference. When this conference united with the Texas-Oklahoma Conference to form the Plymouth Conference of Congregational Christian Churches, title to the property was transferred to the new conference. At the first meeting of the Plymouth Conference, held April 29-May 1, 1948 at the Teche Congregational Christian Church of Morbihan (New Iberia), Louisiana, Edward Phillips was already in declining health, and the conference acted wisely to provide an assistant or temporary director for summer activities at the camp. Funds were appropriated to continue Walter Joseph, of Morbihan, as custodian of buildings and grounds, to put shell on camp roads and pathways, and to make the most urgently needed improvements. The following year the old barracks and other small buildings on the grounds were torn down, and the material from these buildings, supplemented with considerable new materials, was used to erect a new building to provide dormitory space for men and boys, a bath and shower room, and much needed classrooms. A well was dug and a pump was installed, so that for the first time campers were assured of inside toilet facilities and of running water at all times. Before this, a huge cistern, which was wholly dependent upon an abundant rainfall, was the only source of water—for all purposes.

Walter Joseph was highly deserving of credit and praise for

most of the construction work and improvements that took place at Kamp Knighton. For him, as custodian, the Plymouth Conference provided a token "salary" of $25 per month and gave nothing more for his almost full-time services as caretaker, carpenter, plumber, electrician, and handyman. Without him Kamp Knighton could not have operated. Strangely, there was little sickness at Kamp Knighton, but when there was Joseph brought his sister, Nan-Kate, a skilled registered nurse, to attend to the needs of those who were ill.

Franklinton Center has been discussed in earlier chapters. After the move was made from the old Christian College at Franklinton, North Carolina to the more inviting, spacious quarters at Bricks, North Carolina, the place was filled to capacity with summer activities. Ross W. Sanderson, a New Englander noted for his research activities for the denomination, was first president (or director) of Franklinton Center at Bricks. During the few years he was there the old condemned chapel of Bricks Junior College and several small, decaying accessory buildings were torn down and a new home for the president was erected in the center of the campus. Dr. Sanderson had had little experience with Black people, and his ineptness in dealing with southern whites and with ministers and lay leaders of Black churches contributed to his failure as administrator of Franklinton Center. He was followed by William Judson King, a Black minister and the principal of Trinity School, of Athens, Alabama. Dr. King served the center and the Black people in the area of Bricks through the turbulent years of civil rights legislation and racial conflict. The program was expanded. Franklinton Center was one of the few places in North Carolina where Blacks and whites could meet, live, and work together. Interdenominational and interracial church groups, interracial college and university groups, and a variety of social, civic, and religious organizations or groups, together with denominational Black church activities, brought the center into year-round use. Dr. and Mrs. King won the respect and cooperation of the Bricks community; they were welcomed into all the church meetings of North Carolina and of Virginia. Dr. King was sought as guest speaker or preacher by many churches and also served as pastor of the Community Church at Franklinton Center. Mrs. King served as president of the Woman's Fellowship of the Convention of the South for four years. At the time of their retirement, in 1968, the new dining hall that graced the campus stood as a grand monument to their patient, untiring service to Franklinton Center and to the surrounding area.

After Kings Mountain Summer Conference closed, Camp Bessie McDowell, named for the first wife of Henry Curtis McDowell, was organized by the Alabama-Mississippi Conference. Mr. and Mrs. Robert C. Johnson, of Birmingham, were chosen to direct the camp. Mildred Johnson was well known as a leader of girl scouts and Camp Fire Girls; was manager of Sunshine Camp, near Birmingham, Alabama; and was president of the Fellowship of Congregational Christian Women of Alabama-Mississippi. She was the first Black woman to serve as national president of the Fellowship of Congregational Christian Women and later as vice moderator of the General Synod of the United Church of Christ. Camp Bessie McDowell was first held on the campus of Lincoln School, Marion, Alabama. The surrounding hills and woodlands provided opportunities for nature hikes and outdoor cooking and other activities. When the camp was no longer welcome to use the facilities of Lincoln School, it continued its operation at Sunshine Camp, near Birmingham. Through the years, Camp Bessie McDowell enjoyed the capable and enthusiastic leadership of Robert and Mildred Johnson.

Finally, a summer conference or camp for young people from the churches of Georgia and of South Carolina was developed at Dorchester Center, near Midway, Georgia. The director of the center was director and business manager for the camp, which was scheduled for one week each summer. The Rev. A.C. Curtright, of Savannah, the Rev. John T. Enwright, of Charleston, and Dr. Homer C. McEwen, of Atlanta, aided by other pastors and lay leaders, planned and executed an enriched program but also furnished considerable amounts of fruits, vegetables, and seafood, as well as much free labor to keep the camp running smoothly. The beautiful new Midway Church on Dorchester Center grounds offered an attractive setting for vespers and for other worship services. The jungle-like swamps near Dorchester Center were never inviting, but two miles away the historic old antebellum Midway Congregational Church, with its quaint pews and other furnishings and an old cemetery nearby, did invite investigation. All the campers and their adult counselors looked forward to the annual outing on Atlantic beaches. None who spent time at Dorchester Center will forget the Walthours, the Bakers, the Smiths, the Lewises, the Givenses, the Goldens, and the Johnsons, who added enrichment and joy to the experiences at Dorchester Center.

The *ministers' institute* at Franklinton Center was beamed at pastors of North Carolina and of Virginia who had limited educational training. Its major emphasis was in-service training. The *ministers' convocation* was beamed at pastors who had had college and seminary training. It offered a week's refresher experience for ministers who sought to keep abreast of new developments in religion, theology, and pastoral ministry. All its sessions were held either at Talladega College, Talladega, Alabama, or at Interdenominational Theological Center, in Atlanta. It was attended by ministers of the Convention of the South and of the Southeast Convention and was evaluated by them as a worthwhile venture in refresher theological training.

It was my avowed intent that during its first ten years the Convention of the South should become a self-supporting, self-directing conference made up almost entirely of Black Congregational Christian churches. This was no easy undertaking, but it had the full cooperation of most of the ministers and the churches of the convention. Laudable progress was made, and success was reasonably assured. Progress was halted by the union of the Congregational Christian Churches and the Evangelical and Reformed Church, to form the United Church of Christ.

After nearly twenty years of negotiations, in 1957, at a joint meeting of the General Council of Congregational Christian Churches and of the General Synod of the Evangelical and Reformed Church, the United Church of Christ was formed. Then came four more years of legal wrangling. Finally, the General Synod met in Philadelphia and adopted a constitution. With that, the United Church of Christ became an integrated church. The General Synod and all conferences and associations of the United Church of Christ must be inclusive as to race and previous religious and cultural background for *all* within the geographic bounds of these conferences and associations. This inclusiveness was exacting but right and was imperative for any organization that dared to call itself *the United Church of Christ*. But this inclusiveness was the "killer of dreams" for the Convention of the South; the Convention of the South was fragmented by this union.

In this re-forming of the conferences of the United Church of Christ, what became of the Black Congregational Christian churches of the Convention of the South? How were they distributed among conferences of the United Church of Christ? The largest concentration of Black Congregational Christian churches was in North Carolina and in Virginia; there were 155 churches. Of the Black churches in these two states, only thirty were listed as Congregational Christian. When all conferences of the United Church of Christ had been formed, thirty-two of the remaining Black churches of the convention were related to six other conferences of the United Church as follows: Central South Conference, twelve; Indiana-Kentucky, two; Kansas-Oklahoma, one; Missouri, two; Southeast, fifteen. A few Black Congregational Christian churches of the South did not relate to any United Church of Christ conference.

Thus, six conferences of the United Church of Christ share the responsibility and the opportunity of integrating the churches of the old Convention of the South into the life and action of the conference, of giving to them the Christian comradeship and certain assurances that they will sorely need, of sharing with them leadership roles, and of giving them the right to bring into view their own religious experience, their depth of faith, and their spiritual warmth for the enrichment of the life of the conferences and of the United Church of Christ.

Chapter 10

Personalities of the Convention of the South

In the organization and development of all institutions certain individuals stand tall because of their unique personal abilities and contributions, or because of their total loyalty and devotion to the institution itself, or, on occasion, even because of their hostility and opposition toward the institution. In these regards, the Convention of the South of Congregational Christian Churches was no exception. Each of the men I have chosen to lift up was well known and highly respected in his own sphere; each was a minister. Seven were of Christian background; five of Congregational background. All were active during my years as superintendent. All who were chosen are now deceased. These restrictions leave out many, both ministers and lay persons, who played significant roles in the making of the Convention of the South. Some will be mentioned at the conclusion of this chapter. Also, it will be noted that these ministers are listed in alphabetical order, to avoid any suspicion of favoritism.

Simon W. Albright. We knew him as the Rev. S.W. Albright, an old-timer of the Afro-Christian Church, a resident of Raleigh, North Carolina; tall, slender, agile, and of warm black complexion—was always neatly dressed and genteel in manner, and often the mediator, if conflict arose in the church or in the conference. Age had nearly ended his pastoral work, but he was unique as a preacher until the close of his life. It was a privilege to hear him preach, for he knew the Bible; his well-organized sermons were often almost continuous quotes from the Old and the New Testaments, but these quotations were always carefully related to the sermon he was preaching.

Simon Albright died in 1948. There was very little public notice of his death. It was not even possible to get a biographical sketch of his life for the Congregational Christian *Year Book.*

However, those who rejoiced and shouted under the spell of his preaching will always remember this graceful minister of the gospel.

Raleigh Robert Briggs. R.R. Briggs was a Virginian. Born in Windsor, Virginia on November 5, 1897, he was educated in the public schools of Virginia and at the Virginia Union School of Religion. He was ordained by the Black Conference of Eastern Virginia, November 21, 1924, and only in Virginia did he serve as pastor of Congregational Christian churches. His first and longest pastorate (1925–66) was at his home church, in his native town of Windsor; forty-one years was the duration of his entire pastoral ministry. Other Virginia churches that he served were Bethlehem, of Suffolk; Providence, of Norfolk (Chesapeake); and Mount Ararat, of Suffolk. After an extended illness, Raleigh Briggs died in Suffolk, Virginia, January 7, 1967. Thus, practically all his life was spent in Virginia, and all the fruitful years of his life were given to the church and to the Christian ministry.

At some time during his ministry, R.R. Briggs filled every office of his conference; the churches he served were leaders in support of the conference. He was a loyal supporter of the Afro-Christian Convention. He was one of the organizers of the Convention of the South and was a charter member of its board of trustees and an active attendant at all the meetings of the convention. Until his health failed, he championed the cause of the Convention of the South; he attended every ministers' institute at Franklinton Center, encouraged other ministers to do likewise, and always challenged his conference to give scholarships to each conference member-minister who went to the institute.

R.R. Briggs was a true and loyal friend, a good preacher, and an exceptional pastor. Because of a partially invalid first wife, he had become a good housekeeper, a good cook, and a gracious host. At the close of a long trip, a difficult conference, or a church meeting, the rest and renewal needed could always be found in his home.

I was at Franklinton Center, in the ministers' institute, when R.R. Briggs' funeral services were held at Chapel Grove, his home church. The institute closed for the day, and nearly all the ministers at the institute attended the services. The eulogy was delivered by the Rev. Junius O. Lee, a lifelong friend and companion Virginia pastor. Hundreds of people from Virginia and from many places in North Carolina filled the sanctuary and surrounding churchgrounds. They came to honor one of Virginia's most loved and revered pastors.

Arthur Cornelius Curtright. Just as R.R. Briggs was a Virginian, the Rev. A.C. Curtright was a Georgian. He was born in Greensboro, Georgia, and except for his years at the Divinity School of Chicago University, Arthur C. Curtright spent all his years of training and of service in Georgia. For a number of years he taught at Morehouse College, in Atlanta, Georgia. In 1936 he became dean at Savannah State College and continued at this school until 1945. In 1939 he became interim pastor of First Congregational Christian Church of Savannah. The church called no other pastor until he resigned, in 1959. At the time of his resignation the church voted to him the title of pastor emeritus. He remained a loyal member and supporter of the church and of its young pastors until his death, on August 31, 1966.

A.C. Curtright transferred his ministerial standing from the Baptist Church to the Georgia-South Carolina Convention of Congregational Christian Churches in 1945 and later served as moderator of the convention. As moderator, he accompanied me to each church in his association (convention) and acquainted me with many of the problems of his churches and with many of his friends, both in the churches and in the communities we visited. He was a good preacher; a better pastor. He lived in his own home and converted the parsonage into a service center where children, youth, adults, and senior citizens could come for training, service, and recreational activities, as well as for festive occasions. He was eager to show that his community, his church, his home, his lovely wife, and even his luscious vegetable garden were each "as good or better than the best."

A.C. Curtright was gentle and warm-hearted. He was a friend to those in trouble or in need. He was actively concerned with the interracial and civic affairs of his community. He made many personal sacrifices for students, members, friends; he showed compassion for the underdog and was charitable toward his enemies. He often counseled "his superintendent" to be patient with the shortcomings of ministers and of churches and to conserve his own health and energy for a continuing ministry to the Convention of the South. Although his health was fragile after his retirement, A.C. Curtright never failed to serve wherever there was opportunity. When death came, on August 30, 1966, his heart and his home were filled with unfinished tasks that he had assigned to himself. He lived a quiet and beautiful life and left a beautiful legacy to his family, his church, and his friends.

Henderson Hollowell Dunn. The Rev. H.H. Dunn was seventy years of age when I first met him in Louisiana, in 1943. His major accomplishments already were a matter of record. He had served as pastor of Howard, Central, and Morris Brown Congregational churches in New Orleans and of Congregational churches in Baton Rouge and in Schriever, Louisiana. He had served as superintendent of the Louisiana-Mississippi District and as moderator of the Louisiana Association of Congregational Churches. He had been principal of a public school in New Orleans. In 1943 he was still giving pastoral service at the little church at Chacahoula, Louisiana, and this continued until his death, in 1955.

H.H. Dunn was a reporter for the *Times-Picayune,* the daily newspaper of New Orleans. He covered many newsworthy activities and events of interest to Black people. At sessions of the General Council of Congregational Christian Churches he sat in the press section, and his articles appeared regularly in the *Times-Picayune.* He attended all association meetings and summer conferences in his area, and these received generous publicity in his writings. He knew all the churches in Louisiana and the pathways that led to them. During my early years as superintendent he was a wonderful guide and interpreter of Louisiana folkways.

The Dunn family—his wife and five daughters—was noted for its musical and leadership abilities. All six women sang in the choir of Central Church, and most were quite capable of service as pianist or organist for the church whenever needed. They were prominently involved in civic, social, educational, and religious affairs of New Orleans. As director of music in summer conferences and camps, none was more effective with young people or more sensitive to their needs than Florence Ann (Mrs. Swan) at Kings Mountain; or Lillian (Mrs. Perry) at Kamp Knighton. Together they gave Henderson Dunn the companionship and the care that he needed, and often the patient controls required to keep him from overextending himself when excited to action.

For over fifty years Henderson H. Dunn gave of his best in church and educational work. He championed the work of the American Missionary Association and of Congregationalism in the South. He was a loyal promoter of family, community, and church. He died in his beloved city of New Orleans, January 5, 1955.

John Thomas Enwright. The Rev. John T. Enwright was born 1904 in Birmingham, Alabama. After attending the public schools of Alabama he went to Atlanta, Georgia for college and seminary training at Clark College and at Gammon Theological Seminary. He became pastor of First Congregational Church of Athens, Georgia in 1934. Two years later he moved to a rural parish that included the Siloam Church of Hinesville and the Midway Church of McIntosh, Georgia. The year spent in this parish brought to him two experiences that remained with him the rest of his life. One was a very joyous event—the birth of his only child, Florence (Mrs. Miller), who, after graduation from college, came to Charleston to be near her parents until her father's death, November 15, 1975. The other experience was terribly painful and frustrating: the beginning of the attack of a very crippling arthritis on his lovely and capable wife. Mrs. Enwright was never well again. In Greensboro, North Carolina, in New Orleans, Louisiana, and in Charleston, South Carolina the best medical treatment and professional care were secured but to no avail. In Greensboro she worked faithfully with church, Sunday school, and choir but was never without pain for a moment. She continued this activity in New Orleans, and when her physical condition prevented her attendance at church, the Woman's Fellowship and smaller church groups would crowd into her room so that she could share in their meetings. In Charleston a ramp was built from parsonage to church so that she could be wheeled into the church and could enjoy the worship service. Nothing abated her suffering or the worsening of her condition, until death gave the release and the final peace that she so much deserved and desired.

Through all this, John T. Enwright showed marvelous tenderness, patience, and fortitude. He never shirked his home responsibilities; but he never failed his obligations to his church or the opportunities that came for him to serve his community. His ability as a preacher and as a leader became known throughout the Convention of the South. He was twice elected president of the convention, which office he held until the Black churches of the South were merged into conferences of the United Church of Christ. He worked in many youth camps and conferences and ministers' institutes and visited a number of conference (association) meetings; he presided over meetings of the Convention of the South, its board of trustees, and its executive committee with dignity. At all times he showed unusual insight into the problems and needs of the Black churches in the South.

Despite his heart-breaking home experience, John Enwright still had the reserve of strength and of courage to challenge the congregation of Plymouth Church to build a new church of impressive architectural design, to be situated on a spacious new site. When he retired from active pastoral work, he was made pastor emeritus of the church. The new Plymouth United Church of Christ, of Charleston, South Carolina, stands as a monument to him, his church, and its people. From this building his body was carried to its final resting place. He died November 15, 1975 and was buried November 18. He wrote his own epitaph.

Fear no more, the heat of the sun,
Nor the furious Winter's rages;
Thou thy earthly task hast done,
Home art gone, and taken thy wages.

Joseph D. Farrar. The Rev. J.D. Farrar, born November 18, 1879, was a native of Mecklenburg County, Virginia, although for most of his adult years he was a resident of Newport News, Virginia, where he was a member of the Wesley Grove Christian Church. He was ordained November 27, 1912, in Norfolk, by the Eastern Virginia Conference and was called to his first pastorate at Christian Union Church of Newport News. For nearly fifty years he served faithfully the churches of Virginia and of eastern North Carolina, including Mount Ararat and Pleasant Grove in Virginia and Myrtle Grove and Zion Hill in eastern North Carolina.

He also had a tender heart toward the little country church with a waning membership—disheartened and desperately in need of help—such as Homeville or Galatians in Virginia, or Martins Chapel or Pilgrim Rest in North Carolina. When building repairs were needed, he was first to lend a hand. He was no stranger to work and often helped with tasks on the farm or with chores around the homes. He could be content with whatever conveniences or conditions were made available to him. He liked to hunt, he liked to fish, and he liked people. His jovial spirit was contagious. Most of all, he loved his church; he loved to preach and he enjoyed his work as a minister. Underneath his seeming gruffness was a compassion for all who suffered or needed a friend.

For all his years of ministry he was an active and influential leader in the conferences of Virginia and for over twenty years in the Eastern Atlantic Congregational Christian Conference (North Carolina). For twelve years he was president of the Afro-Christian National Convention. He was the first and only treasurer of the Convention of the South. He was faithful and loyal and was present at all services of his churches, at all ministers' institutes, and at most other church-related activities at Franklinton Center. He attended all meetings of his conferences and their auxiliaries, all meetings of the Convention of the South and of its board of trustees, and occasional meetings of the General Council or the General Synod of his denomination. His church was his life.

Joseph D. Farrar, a self-made minister and church leader and a great friend, died April 22, 1967.

Frederick Alexander Hargett was one of the most respected and best loved ministers in North Carolina. He was born in New Bern, North Carolina and became a member of the Christian Church of New Bern. When he was ordained, in 1920, at the Morehead City Christian Church, he had already served for three years as licentiate pastor of this church. After ordination he continued to serve churches of the Eastern Atlantic Christian Conference at Morehead City, New Bern, Pollocksville, and Mariebel. During these pastorates, new church buildings were erected at Morehead City, at New Bern, and at Mariebel. Also during these years he became president of the Eastern Atlantic Conference. He married Florence Hester, who was his lifelong companion both in the home and in his work as pastor. He continued as president of the Eastern Atlantic Congregational Christian Conference for over forty years.

In October 1926 F.A. Hargett was called by St. Stephens Christian Church; he accepted, and the Hargetts moved to Greensboro early in 1927. St. Stephens Church was organized in 1912, when sixty-six members of Bishop's Temple, in protest to demands of the North Carolina Christian Conference, withdrew and organized a new church. These were the sixty-six charter members of St. Stephens. By 1927, however, the membership had declined to thirty-five active members. Frederick Hargett was a good, down-to-earth preacher who was sought by many churches for revivals and special occasions. He was a good organizer and was a wonderful pastor and friend. In times of sickness or distress no member of his church lacked for kindly pastoral ministry. Many an "outcast"—the neglected of Greensboro—could turn to him for sympathetic understanding and help.

When the Stanley family moved to Greensboro in 1943, St. Stephens congregation still worshiped in a small, rundown frame building on High Street. The membership had grown, and the building was crowded to overflowing at almost all morning and evening services. Pastor and church were working desperately to raise money to erect a spacious building on their new church site, just two blocks away. In 1948 the new building was dedicated, and the church reported a membership of 442 and a Sunday school enrollment of 125. The dreams of F.A. Hargett were being fulfilled. The architecture of the church was his own; the building, steel-reinforced throughout and of masonry construction, stood as a monument to his zeal and to his brave determination to build a better church. After forty years of his pastoral ministry and at the time of his retirement, St. Stephens was the largest (682 members) and one of the most actively progressive churches in the Convention of the South.

During the year that I knew him, F.A. Hargett served as president of the Afro-Christian Convention, as president of the Convention of the South, and also as president of the Eastern Atlantic Congregational Conference and of the Lincoln Congregational Christian Conference; as member of the board of trustees of Franklinton Center and of the board of trustees of the Convention of the South. He attended many of the meetings of all conferences in North Carolina and in Virginia and talked persuasively for the success and the support of the convention. At times he and I were accused of looking like brothers and of "eating with the same spoon"; and occasionally, when the going was rough, I reminded him, "You helped get me in this mess; you must help me get through it." For thirty years we were neighbors in Greensboro, never living more than three blocks apart. One could never wished for a better neighbor or a better friend. His death occurred February 16, 1972. It will be difficult to find his equal as a Christian minister and as a loyal leader of Black churches.

Charles Alexander Harris. The Rev. C.A. Harris, born December 12, 1866, had already served his best years as pastor of churches in Virginia and in North Carolina, but he merits listing here. He was one of the three Afro-Christian ministers who supported my election as the superintendent of Negro church work in the Southeast District of the Congregational Christian Churches. Also, he gave excellent pastoral leadership at Laurel Hill Church, Holland, and at Corinth Chapel Church, Franklin, Virginia until 1946. He served the Macedonia Church, in Norfolk, Virginia, as long as he was physically able.

Even in old age, C.A. Harris showed keen insights into the workings and needs of his church. He served in his churches and in the offices of his conferences with dignity and integrity.

148

Even when he required the care and assistance of his wife and his friends, he continued to attend ministers' institutes and other activities at Franklinton Center and to electrify the groups by telling of some of his experiences as a Christian minister. He was staunchly Christian, staunchly Virginian. In his death, on December 1, 1958, Virginia lost one of its oldest and most loyal ministers.

James A. Henderson. The Rev. James A. Henderson was born in Warren County, North Carolina, July 14, 1873. He spent most of his life in Warren County and in adjoining Vance County. On my first trip to Buggs Island (John H. Kerr) Lake, he and I fished in waters that covered the land that once had been his productive farm. Cornstalks still stood along the shores of the lake. The lake was the most recent of the experiences that disrupted his life. For eight years he was president of Franklinton Christian College, one of the schools he attended in his youth and for which he had great dreams. Because the main college building was overcrowded, a new building was started and was moving toward completion. The building was designed to provide a well-equipped kitchen and dining room, storage rooms, offices, and spacious classrooms on the first floor; it was also to include a dormitory for girls and single women on the faculty. But the funds needed to finish the building and to operate the school were dried up at their sources by the Great Depression. The building was never completed; the school closed in the spring of 1930, never to open again.

Then came the merger of Congregational and Christian Churches (1931) and the deal that went through the motion of "merging" Franklinton Christian College and Bricks Junior College and of making J.A. Henderson assistant president of the junior college at Bricks, North Carolina. This was a cruel, traumatic, and disillusioning experience for Henderson. After a few trips to Bricks, where he was not overly welcome, he returned to his farm and to the four rural churches that he served as pastor. He continued to serve these churches—Antioch, Oak Level, and St. Paul, all in Vance County, and Christian Chapel, near Apex, North Carolina.

In his earlier years he had served as pastor of other

149

churches of the North Carolina Christian Conference and as secretary of the conference. He was president of the conference longer than any other minister.

How did J.A. Henderson feel toward his denomination and toward the Convention of the South? I am sure he felt, perhaps with some justification, that he had been let down by his denomination, especially in the negotiations that involved Franklinton Christian College. He was never enthusiastic about the Convention of the South and rarely attended any of its meetings. However, he was president of the largest association in the Convention of the South. To me, as a person, he was always friendly, always courteous, and I never failed to feel welcome in his home, in his churches, and in his conference; he showed little deference for the office of superintendent. He had a keen mind, and he was loved and respected by his people. He was a leader who had to be considered and respected. Thus approached, he gave increasing support to the work of Franklinton Center and even gave token support to the Convention of the South.

James A. Henderson was hurt but was never bitter and hostile. He died March 2, 1961. The Convention of the South and the North Carolina Christian Conference, along with several of its churches, had lost one of the most influential church leaders.

Zanda Pearl Jenkins. The Rev. Zanda P. Jenkins grew up in the Eastern Atlantic (North Carolina) Conference, at Christian Hope, Leland, North Carolina; he was ordained by this association. While receiving his college and seminary training at Shaw University, in Raleigh, North Carolina, he served as a supply pastor in North Carolina. Upon graduation from Shaw University, he moved to Virginia. From 1946 until his death, in 1975, most of his pastoral ministry was with four churches in Virginia: Corinth Chapel, Franklin; Laurel Hill, Holland; Union Christian, Norfolk; and Wesley Grove, Newport News. He was a builder. Each of his churches improved or replaced its building facility, and each grew in membership during his pastorate.

He participated in the interracial and civic affairs of tidewater Virginia. He was active in both of the Virginia conferences and held offices in each. He continued his interest in the Eastern Atlantic Conference, attended all its annual meetings, and served as its secretary for many years. He also attended many meetings of other conferences in North Carolina.

Z.P. Jenkins was elected secretary of the Convention of the South and, by virtue of office, was a member of its board of trustees. Because of his intimate association with all Afro-Christian conferences, in board or convention meetings he could speak intelligently and persuasively to all issues of particular concern for the Afro-Christian churches. Thus, he was of great help to the Convention of the South in keeping a balance of power and in assuring equal consideration and treatment in all segments of the Convention of the South. He was always alert to any problems and needs, always enthusiastic in his support of the convention.

When Zanda Jenkins returned to Wesley Grove Church, his health was seriously impaired, but he persisted in fulfilling his responsibilities to his church. His death was unexpected and untimely. He had driven himself beyond the call of duty, until the fatal heart attack occurred on December 4, 1975.

John Dewey Moore. The Rev. John D. Moore was born February 18, 1904 in Macon, Georgia. He studied at Ballard Normal, a Congregational school in Macon; at Clark College and at Gammon Theological Seminary, both in Atlanta, Georgia; and at Oberlin (Ohio) School of Theology. During his lifetime he held only two pastorates. The first began in 1934, at First Congregational Church, Florence, Alabama. In 1936 he moved with his wife, Frankie, and their first child, Dametta, to Pilgrim Church, Houston, Texas, where he remained until his death, May 11, 1973.

Fire had gutted the Pilgrim church building before he arrived in Houston. Only the charred skeleton remained. Within five years the church had been rebuilt, and a parsonage and garage had been added. A well-kept lawn divided church and parsonage, and John Moore kept a productive vegetable garden in back of the parsonage.

John D. Moore was aggressively active at all times and was involved in many civic and service activities of Houston, in addition to his pastoral work with Pilgrim Church. Around home and church he was a handyman, who often did the job instead of waiting for the janitor to get around to it. A good cook, he delighted in proving his skill. He was an avid photographer, who developed pictures in his own darkroom. As a guest in his home, one could be awakened at almost any hour by the click of typewriter or mimeograph; and one could marvel at the patience and the lovely response of his family to his eagerness for action.

As a leader, he served his own church well. He preached and practiced tithing, planned and directed a program that involved all age levels in a variety of action—choirs, church school, scouting, fellowships for women and men and youth, camping, social service, and community outreach. In his association and at Kamp Knighton Summer Conference he gave full support and excellent leadership. Because he could buy at wholesale prices in Houston, he often brought with him to Kamp Knighton loads of food supplies. He served for several years on the board of trustees of the Convention of the South and urged that a church, as well as its members, should tithe and thus give the needed financial support to the Convention of the South and to the denomination. For a number of years he served on the board of trustees of Huston-Tillotson College, in Austin, Texas.

John D. Moore could not slow down. On my last visit to Houston, Frankie Moore was a delightful hostess in their new home on Rosedale Street. He took pride in showing me his backyard, with its well-built barbecue grill and its possibilities of development for gardening. He then took me on a circuitous trip through his new neighborhood, to the site for the new "church of his dreams." That church was being erected when John D. Moore died, May 11, 1973. He had been stopped in action by a massive heart attack while he was in downtown Houston, "on business as usual."

George Jefferson Thomas. Dr. G.J. Thomas is included not because he played a very significant role in the organization and development of the convention, but because he helped to create the climate for such development. His day was "far spent" when the convention came into being. He had already accomplished his most important work.

Like all the others that are named here, he was a native of

152

the South. He was born August 10, 1878 in Dooly County, Georgia. He was educated at Talladega College and Seminary and later served on the trustee board for that institution. His alma mater honored him with the doctor of divinity degree. He served as pastor of Rush Memorial Church, Atlanta, Georgia; Wentz Memorial Church, Winston-Salem, North Carolina; First Church, Chattanooga, Tennessee; and was interim pastor of Pilgrim Church, High Point, North Carolina. For three years (1921–24) he was field superintendent of Black Congregational churches in Georgia and in the Carolinas. He resigned this work in 1924 to accept a call to Wentz Memorial Church of Winston-Salem. He served this church with distinction for over twenty years. The name of the church—People's Congregational—was changed to Wentz Memorial in honor of the Rev. Samuel F. Wentz, who served as pastor of People's Church from 1921 to the time of his death, February 9, 1924. Wentz had begun the building and had raised it to basement height. This building was completed under the direction of George Thomas. The name of the church was appropriately changed to Wentz Memorial Congregational Church. During his years as field superintendent, Thomas visited all the churches of his district and was respected and loved by ministers and laypeople alike. Under his leadership the membership of the church grew, and the ministry of the church expanded to include a nursery and a day-care center, a kindergarten, and a social work and community program. This program was staffed by well-trained, dedicated persons and won the approbation and financial support of the denomination and of influential people of Winston-Salem. Dr. Thomas' work in Winston-Salem was his most outstanding contribution as minister and pastor.

During most of his years at Winston-Salem, Dr. Thomas was also the moderator of the North Carolina State Conference of Congregational Christian Churches. He probably did more than any other person to determine the future destiny of these churches. At all times he was a forceful preacher; an exacting leader in his church, in his community, and in his conference. He made himself felt and heard wherever he served.

After serving four years as interim pastor of Pilgrim Church, High Point, North Carolina, Dr. and Mrs. Thomas retired to their home in their beloved city of Winston-Salem. Both were in declining health, but they were happy among their friends. Both died within the same week early in 1963. They had given the best years of their lives to the city of Winston-Salem and to Wentz Memorial Church.

I have chosen these twelve, all now deceased, as exemplary of those whose loyalty and dedication to the church made the development of a Black Conference of Congregational Christian Churches in the South a viable possibility. Many others might have been chosen, both living and dead, clergy and laity, men and women, who were no less loyal to the denomination and who were influential leaders among our churches: Junius O. Lee and Robert J. Alston; Susie I. Gregory and Elgin Lowe, of Virginia; Claude C. Simmons and Aurora Taylor; John P. Mangrum and Susie Bullock; William M. Lake, Eddie Hargrove, and Maggie S. Franklin; George Gay Jr., Lula M. Gay, Herbert Howard, and Vina W. Webb; Josephus D. Hill, T.C. Hamans, Ella Cheatham, and Seth T. Shaw, from the associations of North Carolina; Homer C. McEwen, Mrs. M.C. Flipper, and Harold H. Thomas, of Georgia; Harold D. Long, Mildred C. Johnson, and Henry A. Boyd, of Alabama; John Charles Mickle and Aurelius D. Pinckney, of Tennessee-Kentucky; Norman A. Holmes, Corinne Dufour, Elgin Hychew, Walter Joseph, and Dr. L.L. Melton, of the Plymouth Conference, to mention a few.

There were others not as vocal perhaps but no less loyal and dedicated to the work of the Black churches. They too were our friends. All together we were the Convention of the South—a Black Conference of the Congregational Christian Churches and of our own Southland.

Directors of Christian Education
of the
Convention of the South

In addition to ministers and concerned laypersons who worked with the Black churches of the Convention of the South, there were five persons who made significant contributions as directors of Christian education. The work of two others was of such short duration as to make no appreciable impact on the work of the church or on the memory of those who were served. The five were Merlissie Ross Tyson (Mrs. John A. Middleton), Mable Curry (Mrs. Austin), Nezzie V. Carter (Mrs. Moore), Olivia A. Turrentine (Mrs. A.M. Spaulding), and the Rev. Percel O. Alston.

Merlissie Ross Tyson. Merlissie Ross Tyson was employed as assistant director of religious education during the late years of Superintendent Barnwell's administration of Negro church work in the South. She was a native of Mebane, North Carolina, and she and her family were members of the St. Luke Christian Church of Mebane. Thus, she was a natural for her assignment to work among the churches of North Carolina and of Virginia; approximately 80 percent of the Black churches of the two states were Afro-Christian churches. Her assignment to the two states was further indication of the new denominational attitude toward the Afro-Christian churches as a field ripe for church extension and home missionary action. Already I had been appointed director of rural church work in North Carolina and in Virginia. The major portion of my work had been beamed toward the Afro-Christian churches. By October 1, 1942, when I began work as the superintendent of Negro church work in the South, Merlissie Tyson was the only member of the Barnwell staff who remained to work with me.

Before coming into the work as director of Christian education, Merlissie Ross Tyson was trained in the public schools of North Carolina and at Palmer Memorial Institute, of Sedalia, North Carolina. She had graduated with the B.S. degree from Schauffler College of Religious and Social Work, in Oberlin, Ohio. Her training, her geniality, her sensitivity to the religious and emotional needs of the people made her an effective worker in both city and country churches.

I had worked with Merlissie at ministers' institutes, youth camps and conferences, in local conferences and conventions, and in local church situations. She had "a way with people" that made her acceptable at all times. I was fortunate that she remained with me during the initial years of my superintendency. Almost immediately, however, our work was to become a most frustrating experience. As soon as I assumed responsibility as superintendent, Dr. Ernest M. Haliday, who was then general secretary of the church extension division of the Board of Home Missions of Congregational Christian Churches, informed me that no other staff person should be employed, that no office secretary would be provided, and that Merlissie should serve both as director of Christian education and as office secretary. She was quite capable and efficient as director of religious education but had no training or experience in office or secretarial work. As a result, both her work with the churches and the work of the office suffered, with old, well-used equipment from Henry Barnwell's office in Atlanta adding to the problem. I found it necessary to do much of my own typing, and my wife took much of the responsibility for keeping the office open and in operation.

Merlissie worked only in the office and in North Carolina and Virginia, so that I had sole responsibility for all other areas. With these limitations, it was not surprising that she resigned. This resignation became effective December 31, 1943. She was soon married to the Rev. John A. Middleton, a Methodist minister, and had opportunity to continue her keen interest in religious work.

Soon after their marriage the Middletons moved from a parish in Virginia to Atlanta, Georgia, to the pastorate of Allen Temple AME Church. While at Allen Temple their three children—Ann, Johnsy, and Phillip—were born. The elegant new Allen Temple Educational Building and Sanctuary, the new, well-appointed parsonage, the expansion of church program, and the large growth in church membership give glowing testimony to the quality of leadership they gave to Allen Temple.

Merlissie Middleton continued her studies after moving to Atlanta, earning a master's degree at Atlanta University, a certificate in urban studies at George Williams College, and a certificate in African studies at the University of Ghana, West Africa. She has traveled extensively in Europe, Africa, and the Near East. From Allen Temple, John A. Middleton became the president of Morris Brown College, in Atlanta, and served this institution with distinction for many years. Merlissie is associate professor and chairman of the department of sociology of Morris Brown College.

Mable Curry. Merlissie Ross Tyson and Mable Curry were schoolmates at Schauffler College. Merlissie recommended Mable to succeed her as the director of religious education.

Mable Curry, a native of Marion, Alabama, was a graduate of Lincoln High School of Marion, an American Missionary Association school in transition to the public school system of Alabama. From Marion she went to Schauffler College of Religious and Social Work. She came to us, fresh from graduation from Schauffler, with a vigorous enthusiasm for work, especially with the women and the young people. She was untiring in planning and in giving qualified leadership in church activities and in summer conferences and camps. She also gave direction to the student summer service program.

The inadequate salary paid to directors of Christian education made it difficult for us to hold competent persons against more lucratively attractive work. Mable Curry became a school teacher, married, and now lives with her family in Cleveland, Ohio.

Nezzie V. Carter. Nezzie V. Carter, a native of Dudley, North Carolina, was well known to me as a youngster growing up in the Dudley parish. After her father's death, Nezzie, her mother, and brother moved to Durham, North Carolina. She attended the public schools of North Carolina through high school. She too was a graduate of Schauffler College and came well equipped for the work she had chosen.

To many, Nezzie was the "quiet one"—somewhat subdued by harsh childhood experiences of the Depression years but thoroughly dedicated to her work. She prepared very carefully for whatever assignment she was given and ususally carried quantities of materials for distribution among the young people and their leaders. Although she was retiring and avoided speaking in public whenever possible, she planned excellent programs that involved talented young people and many adult leaders in personal participation. Long travel trips became very difficult for her and led to her decision to resign.

157

Nezzie Carter returned to her home in Durham, North Carolina and worked for a time with the YWCA. Later she worked for the public school system of Durham as teacher and counselor in specialized education. She is now married, and her mother lives with her and her husband in their home.

Olivia A. Turrentine. Olivia A. Turrentine, a native of Athens, Alabama, is the youngest daughter of a Congregational minister, the Rev. William J. Turrentine, and is the sister of the first Black Congregational church extension worker, Kathryn Turrentine (Mrs. J. Taylor Stanley). She is part of the fourth generation of a family concerned with the origin and development of Black Congregational churches in the South. The Mary's Grove Congregational Church of Oaks (Mebane), North Carolina was named for her great-grandmother. Her father went from the Oaks community to Talladega for college and seminary training. His first and only pastorate was Trinity Congregational Church, Athens, Alabama.

Olivia attended Trinity, an American Missionary Association school, from kindergarten through high school. Her college work was done at Talladega College. After graduation she returned to Athens and became a teacher in Trinity School.

During college days she worked in the student summer service program and in the youth conferences and became quite popular with children and young people. During her two years of teaching at Trinity School, she was invited to work in the summer conferences and camps at Kings Mountain; Camp Bessie McDowell, Marion, Alabama; and Kamp Knighton, New Iberia, Louisiana. When Kamp Knighton closed, she was persuaded to resign as teacher at Trinity School and to accept an appointment as director of Christian education in the Convention of the South.

As a member of her father's church in Athens, Olivia was active in the youth work of the church and of the Tennessee-Kentucky Conference. While a student at Talladega she participated in the religious activities of the college and of the Alabama-Mississippi Conference. Hence, she was acquainted with many Congregational ministers, young people, and lay leaders. Her religious background gave her immediate rapport with

Black Congregational churches. Her personal warmth and sincere commitment to Christian service made her increasingly acceptable to all churches of the Convention of the South.

Olivia attended all conference, convention, and fellowship meetings of the Convention of the South. She was a forceful, well-informed public speaker and was scheduled to speak at each of these meetings. Behind the scene, she worked to encourage the organization of a woman's fellowship and a youth fellowship in each church. She was a vital force in planning and executing programs for all youth conferences, camps, and retreats. She gave excellent supervision to the student summer service workers, often visiting them in their respective fields, investigating any complaints, and making any adjustments that were needed to improve the service.

Olivia requested a year's leave for study at Andover-Newton Theological Seminary, Newton Center, Massachusetts, but resigned at the end of the following summer and returned to Andover-Newton to complete her graduate study. She has since gone to Hartford Theological Seminary, Hartford, Connecticut, and has earned the Ph.D. degree from this institution.

Olivia is married to the Rev. A.M. Spaulding, a minister of the AMEZ Church and a professor at Hood Theological Seminary, Salisbury, North Carolina. She has been a teacher and director of religious activities at Fayetteville State Teachers' College, Fayetteville, North Carolina; a teacher at Barber-Scotia College, Concord, North Carolina; a teacher and assistant to the president at Livingstone College, Salisbury, North Carolina; and is now dean at Livingstone College.

Percel O. Alston. The Rev. Percel Odell Alston is a native of Virginia and is the son of a Virginia pastor, the Rev. Robert J. Alston. His background has been in the Christian Church, and all his educational training through college was completed in Virginia. His theological training was obtained at Andover-Newton Theological Seminary, Newton Center, Massachusetts. While in seminary he did summer pastoral work at several points in the Convention of the South. After graduation he served for one year as pastor of Midway Congregational Church and as director of Dorchester Center, McIntosh, Georgia.

From Midway he came to the Convention of the South as director of Christian education.

Percel brought a new dimension to the office of director of Christian education in the convention. He was the first male and the first ordained minister to be employed in this position, and also the first of the five to be provided with a motor vehicle for transportation. This relieved me of a great responsibility in providing transportation personally for the director of Christian education, especially to area meetings and to hard-to-reach places. Being a minister, he could supplement his activities with the youth by filling preaching engagements in many churches and at conference and convention meetings. Being a man, he had a direct approach to the men and was successful in organizing and strengthening the Laymen's Fellowship both at local and at convention levels. Percel was quite effective in planning and, in some instances, in directing youth camps and conferences of the Convention of the South. He worked zealously in the Christian education institute that had been established at Franklinton Center many years before by the Rev. Leila W. Anderson. He also organized youth rallies at strategic points in North Carolina and in Virginia. Hundreds of people came to these rallies.

Like other directors of Christian education, Percel lived in my home and shared meals with my family when in Greensboro. This continued until Percel married May Kelly and they bought their own home in Greensboro. All the Stanley children were in college or had completed their college work when Percel came, so that my wife was now free to travel with me on many occasions, especially to summer camps and conferences, local conference and association meetings, and occasionally to national meetings of the denomination. Frequently she served as guest speaker and as resource person for women's organizations and thus relieved Percel and me from an assignment for which we had little aptitude and enabled us to perform more effectively other tasks in the convention that were pressing for attention.

Percel served as director of Christian education of the Convention of the South for eight years. These were turbulent, difficult, transitional years (1955–64) for the denomination and for the Convention of the South. On the one hand, dissident Black church leaders opposed union with the Evangelical and Reformed Church; on the other, the doubtful and even those who gave assent pressed for progress reports, up-to-date information, and documented proof that the union was going forward according to plan and wanted assurance that none of the freedoms and rights of Black Congregational Christian churches would be in jeopardy. Much time was consumed with these interpretations and explanations. A few opposition leaders were quite active and succeeded in holding a number of Black Congregational Christian churches out of the United Church of Christ, stranded alone, with poor pastoral or lay leadership and with no denominational affiliation.

Percel left the Convention of the South to become a staff member for the department of educational resources of the division of Christian education of the United Church of Christ Board for Homeland Ministries. He and May and their three children—Taitu, Karen, and Percel Jr.—moved to Philadelphia, Pennsylvania. Percel has continued with the division of Christian education and has related effectively to Black churches of the United Church of Christ, both north and south. He has prepared a list of all Black congregations and ministers of the United Church of Christ and has served also as coordinator of the national program for Black Church Life and Mission.

Appendix

The ministers listed below served as pastors of churches of the Convention of the South of the Congregational Christian Churches during the years I served as superintendent. Each minister served one or more years as pastor of one or more churches between 1942 and 1965. Only in exceptional instances have ministers of other denominations or clergy who served for short periods as supply pastors been included. The church, or churches, that each minister served are also listed. No attempt has been made to classify the ministers as to conferences or associations, for during this period many served churches in two or more conferences and ministerial standing was frequently moved accordingly. It should also be noted that a number of the older ministers listed had served Black Congregational or Christian churches in the South many years before 1942. Some were already at or beyond retirement age. Likewise, many of the younger pastors listed have come into prominence and have served the Black churches and the denomination significantly.

Albert, Lucius	Carroll Heights, Atlanta, Ga.
Albright, John W.	Archer's Grove, Burlington, N.C.; Holly Springs, N.C.; Poplar Springs, Raleigh, N.C.; St. Luke, Mebane, N.C.
Albright, Simon W.	Mount Zion, Rockingham, N.C.
Alexander, Plummer R.	White's Grove, Norlina, N.C.; Bethlehem, Keats, N.C.; Mount Zion, Henderson, N.C.; Jerusalem, Palmer Springs, N.C.
Alston, Claude D.	Hawfield Chapel, Mebane, N.C.; Neville's Chapel, Chapel Hill, N.C.; Alston's Grove, Chapel Hill,

	N.C.; St. Andrews Chapel, Haw River, N.C.
Alston, James Arthur	Antioch, Suffolk, Va.; Coronado, Norfolk, Va.
Alston, Percel O.	Midway, McIntosh, Ga.; Director, Dorchester Center, McIntosh, Ga.; Director of Christian Education, Convention of the South
Alston, Robert J.	St. Marks, Norfolk, Va.; Zion Bethel, Portsmouth, Va.
Alston, Wavie R.	St. Luke, Goldston, N.C.; Union Grove, McLeansville, N.C.; United, Durham, N.C.; Haw Branch, Sanford, N.C.
Baker, Edward D.	Parish Chapel, Graham, N.C.; Oak Grove, High Point, N.C.; Wesley Chapel, Siler City, N.C.
Banks, Henry B.	First, Anniston, Ala.
Barnhill, Oscar F.	Oak Ridge, Mount Gilead, N.C.; Green Lake, Pekin, N.C.; Strieby, First, Asheboro, N.C.
Bender, William A.	Union, Tougaloo College, Miss.
Blue, Elijah, J.	Maple Temple, Raleigh, N.C.
Boone, Joseph E.	First, Anniston, Ala.; Rush Memorial, Atlanta, Ga.
Boykins, Lewis	Macedonia, Norfolk, Va.; Galatians, Suffolk, Va.; Christian Union, Newport News, Va.; Homeville, Va.
Brice, John	Bethany, Sedalia, N.C.; Wadsworth, Whitsett, N.C.
Briggs, Raleigh R.	Providence, Chesapeake, Va.; Chapel Grove, Windsor, Va.; Mount Ararat, Suffolk, Va.
Bross, John R.	First, Talladega, Ala.
Brown, J.H.	Clinton Memorial, Burlington, N.C.
Brown, James Wiley	First, Corpus Christi, Tex.
Brown, Texas	Christian Union, Newport News,

	Va.; Rising Star, Newport, News, Va.; Corinth Chapel, Franklin, Va.
Brown, Thomas V.	Union Hill, Sedley, Va.; Antioch, Suffolk, Va.; St. Luke, Sedley, Va.; Pocahontas Temple, Wakefield, Va.
Brunston, W.B.	Hawfield Chapel, Mebane, N.C.; Pleasant Union, Raleigh, N.C.
Bullock, Richard D., Sr.	Island Hill, Clarksville, Va.; Ebenezer, Henderson, N.C.
Bullock, Richard D., Jr.	Children's Chapel, Graham, N.C.; Beavers' Chapel, Zebulon, N.C.; Corinth, Youngsville, N.C.; Mount Zion, Henderson, N.C.; Bethleham, Manson, N.C.; Jerusalem, Palmer Springs, N.C.
Burley, Terry J.	First, Chattanooga, Tenn.
Burwell, Joseph M.	Christian Home, Apex, N.C.; First, Cary, N.C.; Spring Street, Wake Forest, N.C.; Zion Temple, Durham, N.C.
Butts, David P.	Hawfield Chapel, Mebane, N.C.; St. Marks, Norfolk, Va.
Calhoun, Nimrod C.	New Emmanuel, Charlotte, N.C.; Gray's Chapel, Statesville, N.C.
Capps, James C.	Liberty Chapel, Moncure, N.C.; Patilla, Burlington, N.C.; McBrooms Chapel, Snow Camp, N.C.; Tempting, Sanford, N.C.
Carter, Clyde J.	Broad Creek, Oriental, N.C.; First, Asheboro, N.C.; Sand Hill, Aberdeen, N.C.; Mount Vernon, Clayton, N.C.
Cash, William L., Jr.	First, Greensboro, N.C.
Cash, William Levi, Sr.	First, Birmingham, Ala.; First, Chattanooga, Tenn.
Cazabatt, Harry H.	Little Zion, Grand Bayou, La.; Mount Horeb, Houma, La.
Christian, G. Chilton	First, Little Rock, Ark.

Coker, Ernest C.	Mount Zion, Rockingham, N.C.; New Rock Spring and Rock Spring, Creedmoor, N.C.; Pope's Chapel, Franklinton, N.C.
Coley, Ronald M.	First, Concord, N.C.; First, Mount Pleasant, N.C.
Copeland, Joseph H.	St. Mary's, Whaleyville, Va.; Zion Bethel, Portsmouth, Va.
Copeland, Joseph M.	Macedonia, Norfolk, Va.; Union Christian, Norfolk, Va.; Zion, Holland, Va.
Cowan, Chal Lee	First, Mooresville, N.C.; Shiloh, Fayetteville, N.C.; Bethel, Statesville, N.C.
Cox, Ben Elton	Pilgrim, High Point, N.C.
Cross, Earl Lee	Salem, Asheboro, N.C.
Cross, Lonnie C.	Lewis's Chapel, Oxford, N.C.; Spring Street, Wake Forest, N.C.
Crutcher, James T.	Evergreen, Beachton, Ga.; Bethany, Thomasville, Ga.
Cunningham, Howard	First, Raleigh, N.C.
Currie, Fred	Christian Chapel, Burlington, N.C.; Burnett's Chapel, Spencer, N.C.
Curtright, Arthur C.	First, Savannah, Ga.; Midway, McIntosh, Ga.
Davidson, Minnie E.	Gray's Chapel, Statesville, N.C.
Davis, Frank J.	Woodbury, Lake Charles, La.
Davis, Thomas, J.	St. John, Addor, N.C.; Ebenezer, Henderson, N.C.
Davis, William J.	Broadway, N.C.; Haw Branch, Sanford, N.C.; Liberty Chapel, Moncure, N.C.; Shinnsville, Troutman, N.C.
Douglas, Vince W.	Midway, McIntosh, Ga.; Director, Dorchester Center, McIntosh, Ga.
Dunlap, Theodore R.	Chandler, Lexington, Ky.
Dunn, Henderson H.	Zion Chapel, Chacahoula, La.; St. Marks, Schriever, La.

Dyer, Jacob A.	Plymouth, Charleston, S.C.
Dyson, Edward J.	First, Meridian, Miss.
Eaton, David H.	St. Paul, New Iberia, La.
Eaton, James A.	Wentz Memorial, Winston-Salem, N.C.
Enwright, John T.	Beecher Memorial, New Orleans, La.; Plymouth, Charleston, S.C.
Ewing, Richard A.	Howard, Nashville, Tenn.
Farmer, James	New Beech Grove, Denbigh, Va.; Rising Star, Newport News, Va.
Farrah, Q.W.	Pine Hill, Siler City, N.C.; Glover's Cross Road, Bennett, N.C.
Farrar, Joseph D.	Galilee, Oriental, N.C.; Pleasant Grove, Littleton, Va.; Mount Ararat, Suffolk, Va.; Zion Hill, Merritt, N.C.; Pilgrim Rest, North Harlowe, N.C.; Galatians, Suffolk, Va.
Faulkner, William J.	Fisk Union, Nashville, Tenn.
Flood, James D.	Piney Grove, Caledonia, Miss.
Foust, Amos T.	Shiloh, Fayettevile, N.C.; Wadsworth, Whitsett, N.C.
Foust, Selma	St. Andrew's, Haw River, N.C.
Fowler, Ulysses S.	First, Talladega, Ala.; Chandler, Lexington, Ky.
Freeman, Lawshee V.	St. Paul, Handsom, Va.; Windsor Grove, Windsor, Va.
Garnett, John E.	Rush Memorial, Atlanta, Ga.
Gates, James R.	Hawfield Chapel, Mebane, N.C.; Sand Hill, Aberdeen, N.C.; Mount Vernon, Clayton, N.C.
Gay, George, Jr.	Gregory, Wilmington, N.C.
Goodman, F.S.	Broad Creek, Oriental, N.C.
Graham, Charles F.L.	Graham, Beaumont, Tex.
Grant, James A.G.	Second, Memphis, Tenn.
Green, William T.	Central, New Orleans, La.
Groves, John W.	Shiloh, Fayetteville, N.C.
Gunn, Oscar F.	Sweet Home, Roanoke, Ala.
Hamans, Thomas C.	Manly Street, Raleigh, N.C.
Hannar, George W.	Melville, Haw River, N.C.; St.

	Luke, Goldston, N.C.; First, Greensboro, N.C.; Liberty Chapel, Moncure, N.C.
Harden, Lloyd	First, Concord, N.C.; Evergreen, Beachton, Ga.; Bethany, Thomasville, Ga.
Hardy, Benjamin E.	Gregory, Wilmington, N.C.
Hargett, Frederic A.	St. Stephens, Greensboro, N.C.
Hargrove, James M., Jr.	Zion Hill, Sanford, N.C.; Island Hill, Clarksville, Va.
Hargrove, James M., Sr.	Elams Chapel, Elams, N.C.; St. Andrew's, Henderson, N.C.; Burchett's Chapel, Manson, N.C.; Roanoke Chapel, Norlina, N.C.; White's Grove, Norlina, N.C.; Mount Vernon, Clayton, N.C.
Harris, Albert S.	Bishop's Temple, Greensboro, N.C.; Sand Hill, Aberdeen, N.C.
Harris, Charles A.	Rocky Branch, Kenly, N.C.; Corinth Chapel, Franklin, Va.; Laurel Hill, Holland, Va.
Harris, James A.	Ebenezer, Henderson, N.C.; Lewis's Chapel, Oxford, N.C.
Harris, James M.	New Bethel, Raleigh, N.C.; Christian Tabernacle, Method, N.C.
Harris, John E.	Oak Ridge, Mount Gilead, N.C.
Harris, Ralph	New Hope, Norfolk, Va.; Antioch, Suffolk, Va.; Bethlehem, Suffolk, Va.
Harrod, B.C.	Calvary, Newport News, Va.
Harvey, Charles T.	Green Level, Haw River, N.C.; Oak Grove, High Point, N.C.; McBroom's Chapel, Snow Camp, N.C.
Hawkins, Obadiah W.	Salem, Asheboro, N.C.
Haywood, Harvey	Christian Tabernacle, Method, N.C.; Antioch, Raleigh, N.C.
Haywood, Seth W.	Galatians, Suffolk, Va.; St. Mary's, Whaleyville, Va.
Hazel, Oscar	United, Durham, N.C.; First,

	Asheboro, N.C.; Tabernacle, Yanceyville, N.C.
Held, John R.	Union, Tougaloo, Miss.
Henderson, James A.	Christian Chapel, Apex, N.C.; Antioch, Townsville, N.C.; Oak Level, Manson, N.C.; St. Paul, Middleburg, N.C.
Henson, Frederic D.	Pilgrim, Okmulgee, Okla.; Second, Oklahoma City, Okla.
Herod, James A.	St. Mary's, Abbeville, La.
Higgs, Nathaniel E.	Rowland's Chapel, Henderson, N.C.; Mount Calvary, Durham, N.C.
Hill, Josephus D.	Eagle Rock, N.C.; New Bethel, Zebulon, N.C.; Saint's Delight, Lewisburg, N.C.; Antioch, Raleigh, N.C.
Hill, William J.	King's Chapel, Alpine, Ala.; Trinity, Athens, Ala.
Hodges, Clifton	Sand Hill, Aberdeen, N.C.; Union Ridge, Burlington, N.C.; Free Liberty, Addor, N.C.; Rocky Branch, Kenly, N.C.; Dry Creek, Candor, N.C.; Liberty Chapel, Moncure, N.C.
Hogan, William E.	First, Montgomery, Ala.
Holland, John Jasper	Holland Mission, Holland, Va.; Green Level, Haw River, N.C.; Broad Creek, Oriental, N.C.
Holloway, George R.	Bethel, Hampton, Va.
Holmes, Norman A.	Central, New Orleans, La.
Holmes, Oliver W.	First, Marion, Ala.; First, Talladega, Ala.; First, Savannah, Ga.
Hood, Nicholas	Central, New Orleans, La.
Hooker, James H.	First, McLeansville, N.C.; McBroom's Chapel, Snow Camp, N.C.; Parish Chapel, Graham, N.C.; Burnett's Chapel, Snow Camp, N.C.; Pleasant Union, Ra-

	leigh, N.C.; Rock Springs, Creedmoor, N.C.; Strieby First, Asheboro, N.C.
Hooker, Percy W.	Shiloh, Fayetteville, N.C.
Hopson, Robert L.	Graham, Beaumont, Tex.
Howard, J.H.	Martin's Chapel, Elizabethtown, N.C.; Zion Hill, Merritt, N.C.; Christian Hope, Leland, N.C.
Jackson, Elijah	First, Anniston, Ala.; Midway, McIntosh, Ga.; Director, Dorchester Center, McIntosh, Ga.
Jackson, John L.	Rush Memorial, Atlanta, Ga.
Jackson, Verdel E.	Midway, McIntosh, Ga.; Director, Dorchester Center, McIntosh, Ga.
Jeffries, William H.	Small's Chapel, Arapahoe, N.C.; Antioch, Maribel, N.C.; St. Matthew's Chapel, Pollocksville, N.C.; Saint's Delight, Lewisburg, N.C.
Jenkins, Zanda P.	First, Dudley, N.C.; First, Franklinton, N.C.; Laurel Hill, Holland Va.; Corinth Chapel, Franklin, Va.; St. Matthew's Chapel, Pollocksville, N.C.; Union Christian, Norfolk, Va.; Wesley Grove, Newport News, Va.
Jeter, R. Hamilton	Gregory, Wilmington, N.C.
Johnson, Edward E.	St. Stephen's, Beaufort, N.C.; Chandler, Lexington, Ky.
Johnson, Fred	St. Stephen's, Beaufort, N.C.
Johnson, Harvey E.	First, Marietta, Ga.
Johnson, Jasper R.	Rand Street, Garner, N.C.; New Bethel, Zebulon, N.C.; Free Liberty, Addor, N.C.
Johnson, Joseph Q.	Bishop's Temple, Greensboro, N.C.; Liberty Chapel, Moncure, N.C.
Johnson, Ned Howard	First, Macon, Ga.
Jones, Alexander M.	Mount Olive and Myrtle Grove,

	Maysville, N.C.; Galilee, Oriental, N.C.; Christian Hope, Leland, N.C.; Zion Hill, Merritt, N.C.; Christian Star, Morehead City, N.C.
Jones, Jiles B.	Pilgrim, High Point, N.C.
Jones, John H.	Rand Street, Garner, N.C.
Jones, Larry N.	Fisk Union, Nashville, Tenn.
Jones, Marion B.	First, Greensboro, N.C.
King, William Judson	Chandler, Lexington, Ky.; Trinity, Athens, Ala.; Bricks Community, Bricks, N.C.; President, Franklinton Center, Enfield, N.C.
Kornegay, L.R.	Bethel, Hampton, Va.
Lake, William M.	Ebenezer, Burlington, N.C.; Children's Chapel, Graham, N.C.; Beulah, Liberty, N.C.; Union Chapel, Burlington, N.C.; Beaver's Chapel, Zebulon, N.C.
Lambert, Augustus G.	Second, Oklahoma City, Okla.
Lawrence, Eugene C.	First, Raleigh, N.C.; First, Franklinton, N.C.
Ledbetter, Caesar S.	Plymouth, Charleston, S.C.
Ledbetter, Theodore S.	Plymouth, Louisville, Ky.
Lee, Cleatus G.	Union Chapel, Burlington, N.C.; Beulah, Liberty, N.C.; Dorsett's Chapel, Spencer, N.C.
Lee, Herman	Zion Hill, Sanford, N.C.; Hickory Grove, Raleigh, N.C.; Pleasant Grove, Raleigh, N.C.; New Rock Spring, Creedmoor, N.C.
Lee, Junius O.	Bethlehem, Suffolk, Va.; Tabernacle, Suffolk, Va.; Bethany, Benns Church, Va.; Small's Chapel, Arapahoe, N.C.
Lee, Willie F.	Lewis's Chapel, Oxford, N.C.; Ebenezer, Henderson, N.C.; White's Grove, Norlina, N.C.
Lewis, G. Franklin	First, Montgomery, Ala.; First, Selma, Ala.

Little, John H.	Kinch's Chapel, Franklinton, N.C.; Pope's Chapel, Franklinton, N.C.; Pleasant Grove, Morrisville, N.C.; Shiloh, Fayetteville, N.C.
Long, Harold D.	First, Birmingham, Ala.
McClam, Edward D.	Rand Street, Garner, N.C.; Maple Temple, Raleigh, N.C.; Rock Spring, Creedmoor, N.C.
McCoy, John D.	First, Asheboro, N.C.; Dry Creek, Candor, N.C.; Collin's Chapel, Robbins, N.C.; Strieby First, Asheboro, N.C.; St. Luke, Goldston, N.C.
McDowell, Henry C.	First, Kings Mountain, N.C.; Principal, Lincoln Academy, Kings Mountain, N.C.
McEwen, Homer C.	First, Atlanta, Ga.
Mack, Edgar L.	Melville, Haw River, N.C.; Bethany, Sedalia, N.C.; Coronado, Norfolk, Va.
McPhatter, J.T.	Zion Temple, Durham, N.C.; Providence, Wise, N.C.; Corinth, Youngsville, N.C.
McRae, Matthew N.	Bear Creek, Robbins, N.C.; Mary's Grove, Mebane, N.C.; Tempting, Sanford, N.C.; First, Troy, N.C.
Mangram, John D.	Union, Tougaloo, Miss.
Mangrum, John P.	First, Cary, N.C.; Beaver's Chapel, Zebulon, N.C.; First, Franklinton, N.C.; Pleasant Grove, Morrisville, N.C.; Hickory Grove, Raleigh, N.C.
Mann, Joseph H.	Union Christian, Norfolk, Va.; Zion, Holland, Va.
Maye, Leslie R.	Plymouth, Dallas, Tex.
Mayfield, Spurgeon J.	Trinity, Athens, Ala.
Meadows, Curtis P.	Cedar Grove, Durham, N.C.; Rowland's Chapel, Henderson, N.C.; Red Hill, Clayton, N.C.; Rocky Branch, Kenly, N.C.

Meadows, John W.	Hickory Grove, Raleigh, N.C.; Pleasant Grove, Morrisville, N.C.
Merritt, James	Pleasant Union, Raleigh, N.C.
Mickle, John Charles	Second, Memphis, Tenn.
Miller, Roy O.	First, Troy, N.C.; St. Stephen's, Beaufort, N.C.
Milteer, James H.	Mount Olive, Maysville, N.C.; Hawfield Chapel, Mebane, N.C.; Pleasant Union, Raleigh, N.C.
Monroe, Robert L.	New Bethel, Raleigh, N.C.; St. John's, Addor, N.C.; Mount Calvary, Durham, N.C.
Moore, John D.	Pilgrim, Houston, Tex.
Moore, Thomas J.	Wesley Grove, Newport News, Va.; Calvary, Newport News, Va.
Morgan, Frank D.	First, Concord, N.C.
Morris, L.J.	Bethany, Sedalia, N.C.; Melville, Haw River, N.C.; Hawfield Chapel, Mebane, N.C.
Morris, Ronald E.	Antioch, Suffolk, Va.
Morrison, James W.	Children's Chapel, Graham, N.C.; First, Troy, N.C.; Green Lake, Pekin, N.C.
Mounts, Lewis H.	First, Macon, Ga.
Paris, Sandy A.	Shinnsville, Troutman, N.C.
Parker, Robert L.	Beecher Memorial, New Orleans, La.; Graham, Beaumont, Tex.
Patterson, Joseph M.	Wentz Memorial, Winston-Salem, N.C.
Pettway, Thomas H.	Antioch, Townsville, N.C.
Phillips, Edward H.	Teche, New Iberia, La.; Director, Kamp Knighton, New Iberia, La.
Pinckney, Aurelius D.	Second, Memphis, Tenn.; Plymouth, Louisville, Ky.
Poe, Denmark L.	Washington Terrace, High Point, N.C.; Shiloh, Fayetteville, N.C.; Strieby First, Asheboro, N.C.
Price, Jonah	Homesville, Va.
Rasberry, Hosea	Graham, Beaumont, Tex.

Robertson, Burnell J.	St. Paul and Teche, New Iberia, La.
Routte, Thomas L.	First, Marion, Ala.
Ruffin, Ott T.	Ruffin Chapel, Burlington, N.C.
Samuels, Charles W.	Dry Creek, Candor, N.C.; Liberty Chapel, Moncure, N.C.; Mount Zion, Rockingham, N.C.
Scott, Hosea	Holland Mission, Holland, Va.; St. Paul, Handsom, Va.; Pleasant Grove, Littleton, Va.
Sheares, Reuben A., II	Howard, Nashville, Tenn.
Sherrod, Robert D.	Beecher Memorial, New Orleans, La.
Shipman, Russell J.	First, Kings Mountain, N.C.; First, Troy, N.C.
Simmons, Claude C.	Christian Star, Morehead City, N.C.; West Street, New Bern, N.C.; Christian Chapel, Stella, N.C.
Simmons, Handy O.	Emmanuel, Kinston, N.C.; Mount Olive, Maysville, N.C.; Broad Creek, Oriental, N.C.; Small's Chapel, Arapahoe, N.C.
Simmons, William E.	Washington Terrace, High Point, N.C.; First, Asheboro, N.C.; Mount Zion, Rockingham, N.C.
Skeeter, Romie R.	Windsor Grove, Windsor, N.C.
Smith, Andrew J.	Mount Zion, Dover, N.C.
Smith, Delaney G.	First, Dudley, N.C.
Smith, Hardeman D.	First, Asheboro, N.C.; Washington Terrace, High Point, N.C.
Smith, Sidney R.	First, Corpus Christi, Tex.
Spearman, Elvis W.	Evergreen, Beachton, Ga.; Bethany, Thomasville, Ga.
Steed, Matthew C.	Zion Hill, Sanford, N.C.; Kinch's Chapel, Franklinton, N.C.; Maple Temple, Raleigh, N.C.
Stoudt, John J.	First, Talladega, Ala.
Thomas, George	Coronado, Norfolk, Va.

Thomas, George J.	Wentz Memorial, Winston-Salem, N.C.; First, Chattanooga, Tenn.; Pilgrim, High Point, N.C.
Thomas, William H.	Rock Spring, Creedmoor, N.C.; Kinch's Chapel and Pope's Chapel, Franklinton, N.C.; Parish Chapel, Graham, N.C.; Mount Zion, Dover, N.C.; St. Matthew's Chapel, Pollocksville, N.C.; First, Jacksonville, N.C.; Antioch, Maribel, N.C.; Beulah, Liberty, N.C.; Zion Hill, Merritt, N.C.
Thompson, Charles L., Sr.	Union, McLeansville, N.C.; St. Andrew's, Haw River, N.C.; Collin's Chapel, Robbins, N.C.
Threadvill, Thomas L.	First, Marion, Ala.
Traylor, H.L.	First, Chattanooga, Tenn.
Trescott, Clarence B.	First, Dudley, N.C.
Truesdell, Henry L.	Bethel and Gray's Chapel, Statesville, N.C.
Upton, Clarence E.	New Hope, Norfolk, Va.
Upton, Milton L.	Rush Memorial, Atlanta, Ga.; Beecher Memorial, New Orleans, La.
Vallier, A.	St. Mary's, Abbeville, La.; Beard, Erath, La.
Walden, Henry R. (retired)	Broadway, N.C.
Walker, Abraham L.	First, Talladega, Ala.
Walker, Charles C.	First, Meridian, Miss.; First, Little Rock, Ark.
Walker, Samuel L.	Calvary, Newport News, Va.; Macedonia, Norfolk, Va.
Ward, Andrew J.	Jones Chapel, Moncure, N.C.; Hank's Chapel, Pittsboro, N.C.
Washington, Arthur G.	Woodbury, Lake Charles, La.
Washington, N.	Macedonia, Norfolk, Va.
West, James B.	First, Dudley, N.C.
White, Benjamin F.	People's and Plymouth, Dallas, Tex.

White, Leon	Christian Chapel, Apex, N.C.; Antioch, Maribel, N.C.; Galilee, Oriental, N.C.; Oak Level, Manson, N.C.
Whitt, Booker T.	Belle, New Iberia, La.; Beard, Erath, La.; Hubbard, Gueydan, La.
Williams, Carlyle	Spring Street, Wake Forest, N.C.
Williams, George A.	Central, New Orleans, La.
Williams, Lloyd	St. Mary's, Abbeville, La.; Teche, New Iberia, La.
Williams, Milton	Gregory, Wilmington, N.C.; First, Birmingham, Ala.
Wright, Andy	Glover's Cross Road, Bennett, N.C.; Clinton Memorial, Burlington, N.C.
Wright, John C.	First, Atlanta, Ga.
Young, Andrew J.	Evergreen, Beachton, Ga.; Bethany, Thomasville, Ga.
Young, Lonnie C.	St. John's and Free Liberty, Addor, N.C.; Zion Hill, Sanford, N.C.
Young, Thomas	Rowland's Chapel, Henderson, N.C.

CPSIA information can be obtained
at www.ICGtesting.com
Printed in the USA
LVHW091029231221
706632LV00037B/688

9 780829 818369